The

Southern Way

The regular volume for the Southern devotee

Peter Waller

Issue 72

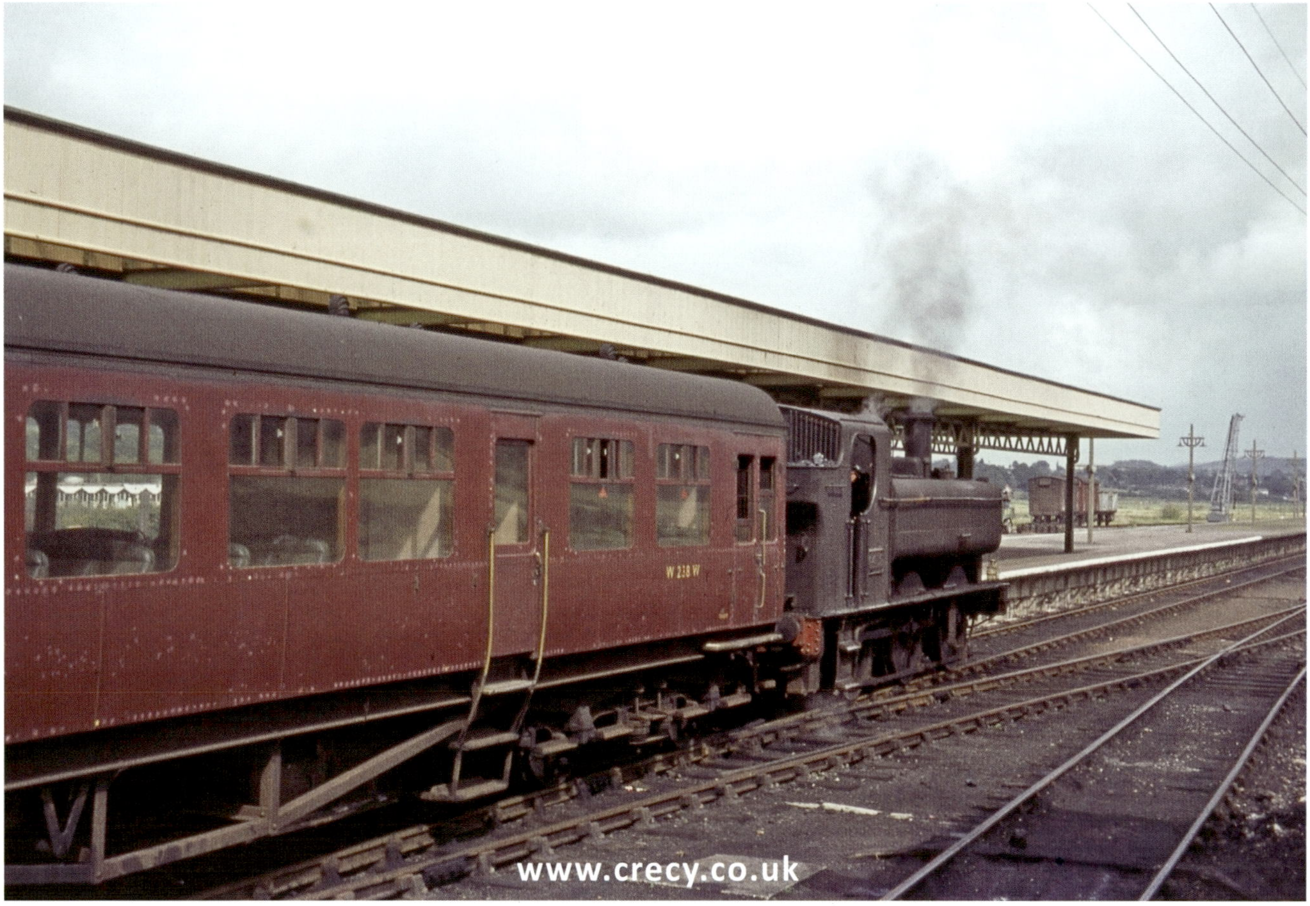

ISBN 9781800353558

First published in 2026 by Crécy Publishing Ltd

Contact details
All editorial submissions to:
The Southern Way
Crécy Publishing Limited
1a Ringway Trading Estate
Shadowmoss Road
Manchester M22 5LL
enquiries@crecy.co.uk

A CIP record for this book is available from the British Library

Publisher's note: Every effort has been made to identify and correctly attribute photographic credits. Any error that may have occurred is entirely unintentional.

Printed in the UK by ESP Colour

Crécy Publishing Limited
1a Ringway Trading Estate
Shadowmoss Road
Manchester M22 5LH

www.crecy.co.uk

Front cover:
On 13 November 1982 Class 508 No 508019 is seen approaching Wimbledon with the 12.46 service from Waterloo to Shepperton. In the background, Class 4VEP No 7715 makes its way westbound with the 12.50 to Guildford. No 508019 was one of the 12 units that were to return to the Southern post-privatisation, becoming Connex No 508208. It was one of the class that survived in service until final withdrawal in December 2008.
Bernard Harrison/Bob Bridger Collection/Online Transport Archive

Back cover:
The oldest type of ex-Southern Railway class to remain operational — and the only pre-grouping design to survive into 1966 — was the 'O2' 0-4-4T, of which 13 were based on the Isle of Wight. Here No W27 *Merstone* is seen at Shanklin on 6 July 1966.
John Worley/Online Transport Archive

Title page:
In May 1963, ex-GWR 0-6-0PT No 6412 awaits departure from Seaton with the push-pull service to Seaton Junction. The train comprised two autotrailers with No W238W leading. See the article on the Seaton branch on page 35.
Phil Tatt/Online Transport Archive

Contents

Issue No 73 of THE SOUTHERN WAY
ISBN 9781565812314
available in May 2026 at £14.95

To receive your copy the moment it is
released, order in advance from your usual
supplier, or it can be sent post-free (UK)
direct from the publisher:

Crécy Publishing Ltd

1a Ringway Trading Estate, Shadowmoss
Road, Manchester M22 5LH

Tel 0161 499 0024

www.crecy.co.uk

enquiries@crecy.co.uk

Introduction

As this issue of *Southern Way* is being put together, one of the stalwarts of Southern operation over the past four decades is about to bow out. It is frightening to recall that the Class 455 EMUs were first introduced in 1983; over the past 40 years they were a familiar sight on suburban services on the South Western and South Central. A total of 137 units were delivered from BREL's Holgate Road Works in York between 1982 and 1985; these included a total of 505 newly built carriages that were supplemented by utilising 43 trailer cars transferred from the Class 508 stock when the latter were converted to three-car units for use on Merseyside; the slightly different profile of the ex-Class 508 carriages gave the 43 Class 455/7 units a slightly odd look — vaguely reminiscent of older trains when stock with differing roof profiles were much more common.

Over the years, the Class 455s proved themselves to be reliable carriers of vast numbers of commuters on the suburban services which they operated. Relatively simple compared to the complexity of much of the more modern rolling stock delivered over recent decades, the class regularly featured amongst the winners of the Golden Spanners Award, promoted by *Modern Railways*, for the most reliable trains — indeed, they were to again achieve that accolade in the awards announced in November 2025. Few, I imagine, would have contemplated such a long operational life when they were

completed but regular refurbishment and issues with the proposed replacement stock resulted in a longevity that again reflects well on the inherent strength of the original concept.

There were issues with them; overcrowding — an issue not only with this class as passenger traffic increased over the years — in the peak hours made them uncomfortable the closer you got to London; my relatively infrequent trips into and out of London in peak hours made me pleased that I never had to do the commute on a regular basis. Designed for suburban services, the units lacked lavatories; this was never a problem over short journeys but with trips that could be almost an hour or more — such as Waterloo to Shepperton — this was also not always comfortable.

As the class finally gives way to the new Class 701s, we can say farewell to a long and faithful servant. Whether its successors will last anywhere near as long must be open to some doubt. Over the years the Class 455s have certainly merited the investment made in them; it's unlikely we'll see their like again.

Peter Waller

On 26 May 1990, Class 455 No 5913 is pictured at Vauxhall with a Down service to Dorking. This was one of 20 Class 455/9s delivered during 1985; the last of this batch were scrapped in late 2025. *Peter Waller*

Southern Steam Survivors

Of the less than 100 survivors, more than half were Bulleid Light Pacifics, the majority of which had been rebuilt. On 13 September 1966, No 34034 *Honiton* was pictured at Banbury with the last Down Poole to York service to operate via the Great Central main line.
Geoffrey Tribe/Online Transport Archive

Sixty years ago — in January 1966 — steam operation on the Southern Region was entering its final full year. It had disappeared from the South Eastern and South Central leaving the South Western as its last redoubt, in particular the main line from Waterloo to Bournemouth and Weymouth. Work, however, on this route to facilitate steam's replacement by diesel and electric traction was proceeding apace. Whilst countless withdrawn locomotives were to be found in scrapyards awaiting their fate, less than 100 steam locomotives that had their origins with the Southern remained in service allocated to a handful of sheds — Bournemouth, Eastleigh, Guildford, Nine Elms, Ryde, Salisbury and the ex-GWR Radipole shed in Weymouth plus Templecombe and Bath Green Park on the Somerset & Dorset (which were now controlled by the Western Region) and others, such as Basingstoke, which had lost their allocation but which remained active as a servicing point — and this number would have been even smaller if the planned closures on the Isle of Wight had not been deferred from 1965 until the following year. In addition to the ex-Southern locomotives, the surviving steam services on the Southern also relied upon a number of the BR Standard classes.

34066

35008
JENKIN

Only three examples of Bulleid's Class Q1 survived into 1966; these were Nos 33006, 33020 and 33027. The oldest of this trio is pictured here on 30 December 1963 in use shunting at Dorking Town. *Neil Davenport/Online Transport Archive*

Opposite top: **Recorded on the same day, but at Oxford, was unrebuilt 'Battle of Britain' No 34066** *Spitfire* **with the 8.30am Saturdays Only service from Manchester to Poole; this again had historically operated via the Great Central and was travelling via the route for the final time.** *Geoffrey Tribe/Online Transport Archive*

Bottom: **More than half of the 'Merchant Navy' class remained operational at the start of the year but this number was to be reduced by six during the course of 1966 with Nos 35010/11/17/22/27/29 all succumbing during the 12 months. No 35008** *Orient Line* **— seen here arriving at Southampton Central with the 9.54am service from Weymouth to Waterloo on 18 September 1966 — was one of only 10 to survive into 1967.** *Charles Firminger/Bob Bridger Collection/Online Transport Archive*

Another type reduced to a handful on 1 January 1966 was the 'U' class 2-6-0. Four survived into 1966 — Nos 31639, 31791, 31803 and 31809 — and here No 31639 is pictured at Bentley on 9 January 1966 prior to working the Bentley-Borden and return section of the LCGB 'S15 Commemorative' rail tour. The original excursion was booked to operate on the 16th; however, such was the demand for tickets that a repeat tour was operated the previous week. Allocated to Guildford when recorded here, No 31639 was not to survive for much longer; it was withdrawn in early June 1966.
Charles Firminger/Bob Bridger Collection/Online Transport Archive

Although officially withdrawn from service in mid-September 1965 from Feltham, where it had been based from January that year when it had been reallocated from Eastleigh, Class S15 No 30837 was returned briefly to Feltham shed in early 1966 so that it could provide the motive power for the two LCGB organised 'S15 Farewell' rail tours in January 1966. A few days before the running of the first special, No 30837 was used on a test run as it had been unused since its official withdrawal date. Following the running of the second of these trains, on the 16th, the 'S15' was again taken out of service; there was to be no further reprieve — it was scrapped at Cashmore's of Newport eight months later.
Charles Firminger/Bob Bridger Collection/Online Transport Archive

The delayed closure of the lines on the Isle of Wight also resulted in a temporary reprieve for the Class O2 0-4-4Ts with 13 operational at the start of the year. Amongst the survivors was No W35 *Freshwater*, which is seen here departing from Ryde Pier Head station on 6 July 1966.
John Worley/Online Transport Archive

Acquired by the Southern in 1947 just prior to nationalisation were the 14 Class USA 0-6-0Ts that had been purchased to replace the older Class B4 tanks for operation on the lines that served Southampton docks. Largely superseded by the future Class 07 diesel shunters, by the start of 1966 10 remained with BR; of these four were in departmental use by this date. On the occasion of both of the 'S15 Commemorative' railtours of 9 and 16 January 1966, No 30073 was employed to haul the special from Eastleigh station into the works and return. The surviving locomotives were Nos 233 (ex-30061), DS234 (ex-30062), 30064, DS237 (ex-30065), 30067, 30069, DS238 (ex-30070), 30071-73. Although a number of the class survive in preservation, No 30073 was not so fortunate; withdrawn in January 1967, it was scrapped at Cashmore's in Newport during June 1967.
Charles Firminger/Bob Bridger Collection/Online Transport Archive

Somerset & Dorset
The Last Weekend

Sixty years ago, in the knowledge that the Somerset & Dorset line was scheduled to be officially closed from Monday 7 March 1966, four specials — two on the Saturday and two on the Sunday — operated over the route alongside the normal timetabled services. On the Saturday the Locomotive Club of Great Britain (LCGB) ran its 'Somerset & Dorset' rail tour from Waterloo whilst the Great Western Society operated a return special from Bournemouth to Bath Green Park. On the 6th a second special was operated from Waterloo; this was the 'Somerset & Dorset Farewell' organised by the Railway Correspondence & Travel Society. The final special — promoted by the Midland Area branch of the Stephenson Locomotive Society — was billed as the last passenger train on the Bath to Bournemouth via Templecombe section.

The locomotive employed on the Waterloo to Templecombe special and the return — from Bournemouth on the Saturday and from Templecombe on the Sunday — was 'Merchant Navy' No 35028 *Clan Line.* **The Pacific, bearing its LCGB headboards, is pictured awaiting departure from Waterloo on 5 March 1966.** *Charles Firminger/Bob Bridger Collection/Online Transport Archive*

A sign of the times: the official closure notice, suitably, if unofficially, decorated to mark the final weekend of the Somerset & Dorset's operation. *Graham Holt/Online Transport Archive*

On both days, the 'Merchant Navy' took the special as far as Templecombe on the outbound journey. Pictured at Templecombe prior to being removed from the train, the locomotive had been on time for the entire 112 miles from Waterloo; the booked arrival time at Templecombe — 11am — was met with 20 minutes allowed for in the timetable to effect the switch of locomotives. *Charles Firminger/Bob Bridger Collection/Online Transport Archive*

Opposite top: Two Ivatt-designed 2-6-2Ts — Nos 41249 and 41307 — were rostered for the section from Templecombe to Evercreech Junction and to Highbridge plus the return from Highbridge to Evercreech Junction. Recorded here at Templecombe shortly before departure, the train departed at 11.19am, one minute ahead of schedule. *Charles Firminger/Bob Bridger Collection/Online Transport Archive*

Bottom: The two Ivatt tanks ran round the train at Highbridge following its arrival at 12.35pm, 10 minutes ahead of schedule.
Charles Firminger/Bob Bridger Collection/Online Transport Archive

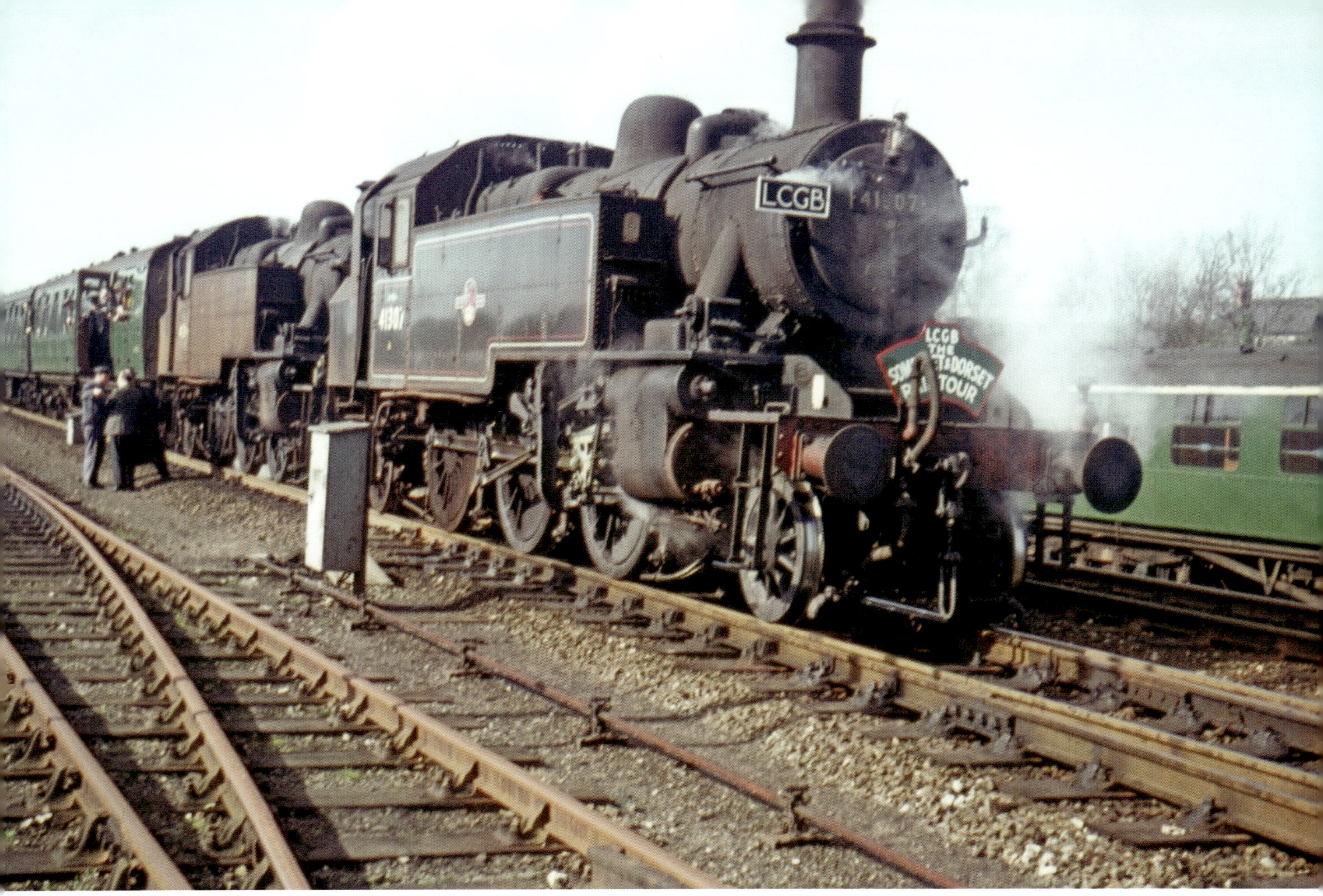
LCGB
LCGB
THE
RAIL TOUR
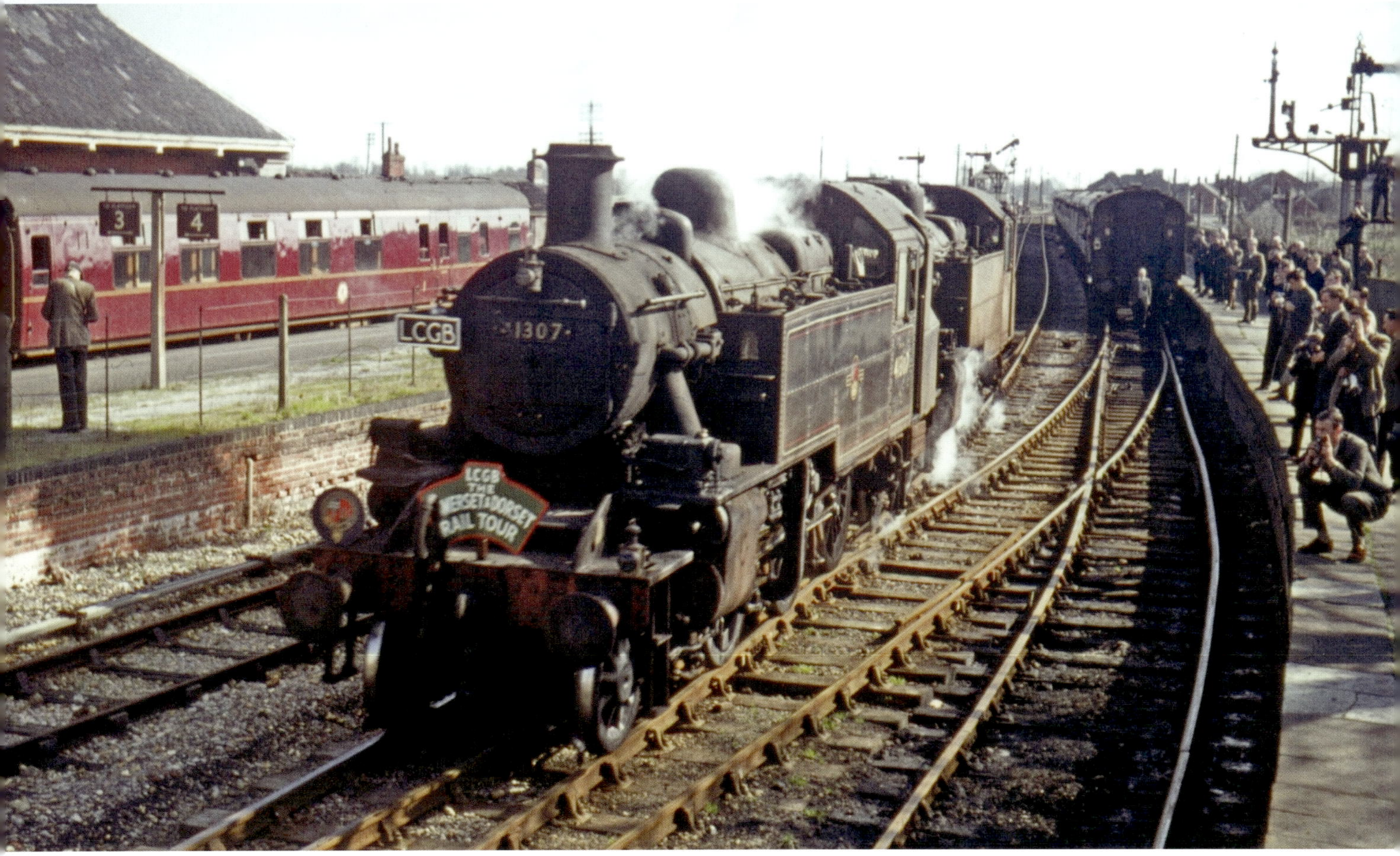
3
4
LCGB
1307
LCGB
THE
RAIL TOUR

Now turned and watered, the two Prairies are seen prior to departure on the return working to Evercreech Junction. Although the special had arrived at Highbridge early, it was not until 1.13pm — eight minutes late — that the return journey commenced.
Charles Firminger/Bob Bridger Collection/Online Transport Archive

Opposite top: **Prior to departure, both locomotives were turned on the turntable at Highbridge; here No 41249 is pictured. Completed at Crewe Works in November 1949, the locomotive spent much of its operational life based on the S&D, including two periods when it was allocated to Templecombe (from the summer of 1953 through to January 1959 and from June 1965 onwards). Looking in poor external condition, the 2-6-2T was one of the locomotives withdrawn as a consequence of the line's closure.** *Charles Firminger/Bob Bridger Collection/Online Transport Archive*

Bottom: **Recorded alongside the water tower is No 41307 looking in much better fettle than its sister, although it was also to be a victim of withdrawal once the S&D was no more. Built at Crewe in April 1952, the locomotive had been allocated when new to Three Bridges before being reallocated to Exmouth Junction during the summer of 1955; it was a relatively late arrival on the S&D scene, having been transferred to Templecombe exactly a decade later.** *Charles Firminger/Bob Bridger Collection/Online Transport Archive*

At Evercreech Junction, two Bulleid Pacifics — Nos 34006 *Bude* and 34057 *Biggin Hill* — were rostered to take the train north to Bath Green Park; here the pair are recorded prior to departure. Although the train had been late leaving Highbridge, it had caught up time by its arrival at Evercreech Junction and was to depart at 2.5pm — five minutes early. *Charles Firminger/Bob Bridger Collection/Online Transport Archive*

Opposite top: No 34006 looked in excellent external condition as it took over the special at Evercreech Junction; based at Nine Elms for the bulk of its BR career, the 'West Country' had been transferred to Salisbury in the later summer of 1964. It was to remain allocated there until withdrawal in mid-March 1967. *Charles Firminger/Bob Bridger Collection/Online Transport Archive*

Bottom: Following the special's arrival at Bath Green Park, 0-6-0PT No 3681 — bereft of its cabside numberplates — was employed to remove the ECS to permit the locomotives to access the shed. The Collett design locomotive, new from Swindon in July 1940, had been transferred from South Wales to Bath Green Park in the autumn of 1964. Its poor external condition is again, perhaps, indicative of its short-term fate — it was another locomotive withdrawn immediately after the closure of the line. *Charles Firminger/Bob Bridger Collection/Online Transport Archive*

80039
48444
48444

34006
LCGB
LCGB THE SOMERSET & DORSET RAIL TOUR
XP

Alongside the specials, the regular timetabled service was also operated. Here Standard 2-6-4T No 80138 and Ivatt 2-6-2T No 41307 are pictured arriving at Green Park with the 2pm service from Templecombe. The Ivatt, fresh from its exertions earlier in the day, had been attached at Evercreech Junction. No 80138 had been based at Neasden when new in June 1956, but was reallocated to Tunbridge Wells West at the end of 1959. Based at Brighton from early 1961 and Redhill from early 1964, the locomotive was transferred to Bournemouth early the following year. Whilst not withdrawn with the closure of the S&D, it was not to survive much longer, being taken out of service at the start of October 1966.
Charles Firminger/Bob Bridger Collection/Online Transport Archive

Opposite top: **Pictured on shed — but already withdrawn — was Class 8F No 48444. A much travelled example of the class — it had been based at Agecroft, Mold Junction, Westhouses, Pontypool Road (twice), Shrewsbury, Chester West, Tyseley, St Philip's Marsh and Llanelly before its move to Bath Green Park in July 1964 — the 2-8-0 had been withdrawn in mid-February 1966. It was not to survive much longer, being scrapped at Newport in April 1966. It is pictured alongside another withdrawn locomotive — Standard 2-6-4T No 80039 — which had been taken out of service from Templecombe in January 1966; this was scrapped at Newport in March 1966.** *Charles Firminger/Bob Bridger Collection/Online Transport Archive*

Bottom: **Prior to heading the return working to Bournemouth, No 34006 is seen taking on water at Green Park.**
Charles Firminger/Bob Bridger Collection/Online Transport Archive

Another Standard 2-6-4T recorded in steam at Green Park was No 80043. Transferred to Templecombe from Exmouth Junction in the early autumn of 1964, the locomotive was not to remain operational for much longer; it was officially withdrawn on Monday 7 March 1966. It was also to meet its fate — in July 1966 — at Cashmore's yard in Newport. *Charles Firminger/Bob Bridger Collection/Online Transport Archive*

Opposite top: 'Battle of Britain' No 34057 *Biggin Hill*, having been watered, was the first of the two Pacifics to be reattached to the special. Based at Salisbury from September 1963, the Pacific was, when withdrawn in early May 1967, the last remaining Unrebuilt Bulleid Pacific still in operation. *Charles Firminger/Bob Bridger Collection/Online Transport Archive*

Bottom: On the return journey to Templecombe, the special made an unscheduled stop at Shepton Mallet for photographs to be taken. By this stage the special was already running late; it had been scheduled to pass through the station at 4.37pm but, in reality, stopped there from 4.54pm for seven minutes. *Charles Firminger/Bob Bridger Collection/Online Transport Archive*

It was not only Green Park shed that closed with the line; another casualty was the shed at Templecombe, pictured here with Ivatt 2-6-2T No 41283 over the fateful weekend. The two-road shed had been rebuilt by BR in 1951 in brick, with a steel frame and asbestos roof. *Graham Holt/Online Transport Archive*

Opposite top: **Pictured heading southbound at Wincanton with the SLS special on the Sunday — announced as the last passenger train on the line — are Class 8F No 48706 and Standard 2-6-4T No 80043. The '8F' was allocated to Bath Green Park, having been transferred from Llanelly in June the previous year, whilst No 80043 had been based at Templecombe since October 1964; this special was probably the last duty for both of them as the pair were withdrawn following the closure of the S&D.** *Charles Firminger/Bob Bridger Collection/Online Transport Archive*

Bottom: **The SLS special also traversed the section from Templecombe No 2 Junction into Templecombe station and return on its southbound journey. For the return working the 10 coaches — plus Nos 48706 and 80043 (which were booked for the full working to Bournemouth and back) — were hauled to Templecombe No 2 Junction by Ivatt 2-6-2T No 41249. The train is seen here approaching No 2 Junction just after 12.36pm (some 10 minutes late). Templecombe-allocated No 41249 was another victim of the line's closure.** *Charles Firminger/Bob Bridger Collection/Online Transport Archive*

Having spent the day chasing the SLS special, Roy Hobbs captured a couple of service trains at Wincanton. The first of these — heading southbound — was hauled by Standard 2-6-0 No 76026. Delivered new to Eastleigh in October 1953, the 2-6-0 had been transferred to Bournemouth in August 1961; it was to survive the closure of the line by more than a year, being one of the class to survive until the end of SR steam in July 1967. *Roy Hobbs/Online Transport Archive*

Heading north was Class 8F No 48760 at the head of a three-coach train to Bath. No 48760 was one of the class to be transferred from Llanelly during 1965 — this case in August — to Bath Green Park. The LNER-built locomotive had spent the bulk of its BR career based on the Western, including more than seven years allocated to Shrewsbury. Following the closure of the S&D, the '8F' was withdrawn. *Roy Hobbs/Online Transport Archive*

On 5 March 1966 the Great Western Society also organised a special; this was run from Bournemouth to Bath Green Park and return with Class 8F No 48706 booked to haul the service in both directions. The train is pictured here near Chilcompton. Another of the class to migrate from Llanelly to Bath Green Park — this time in June 1965 — No 48706 was also to fall victim to the line closure, being withdrawn after the weekend. *Roy Hobbs/Online Transport Archive*

The RCTS sponsored 'Somerset & Dorset Farwell' tour on 6 March 1966 was hauled from Waterloo to Templecombe No 2 Junction, via Bournemouth Central and Broadstone, by 'Merchant Navy' No 35028; the Pacific was then replaced by two Ivatt 2-6-2Ts — Nos 41249 and 41283 — for the run to Highbridge. At Highbridge (S&D) station the passengers disembarked whilst the train ran ECS into the GWR station with passengers walking between the two. Once fully loaded, the special then took the GWR main line via Bristol to Bath Green Park. For this section of the tour, the train was hauled by No 34013 *Okehampton*. *Charles Firminger/Bob Bridger Collection/Online Transport Archive*

The Brighton Atlantic Tanks

Douglas Earle Marsh had, prior to his appointment as Locomotive, Carriage and Wagon Superintendent of the LBSCR in November 1904, served as Assistant Works Manager at Swindon and, from 1896, as Chief Assistant Mechanical Engineer to Henry Ivatt on the Great Northern Railway (GNR). Whilst with the GNR he had worked closely with Ivatt on the design of that railway's Atlantic classes. It was, perhaps, inevitable that he would bring that experience to bear when designing locomotives for his new employers; of the designs that he produced, six were for Atlantic types, including four classes of 4-4-2T predominantly for use on the railway's suburban services.

The first of these to emerge was the 'I1' class in September 1906 with the completion of No 595 at Brighton. As built, this initial locomotive differed from the subsequent 19 built. The remainder of the class were constructed at Brighton between November 1906 and December 1907. Intended to haul secondary passenger services — primarily in the south London suburbs — the class proved unsuccessful, being notorious for their poor steaming (a result of the small fireboxes with which they were equipped) although they were reliable. The first three to be completed, Nos 595-97, had a smaller water capacity than the remainder of the class (1,839 gallons as opposed to 1,924). The last 10 to be constructed — Nos 1-10 — reused the motion and wheels from recently withdrawn Stroudley-designed Class D1 and D2 0-4-2s; this resulted in a reduction of the wheelbase from the 8ft 9in of the original 10 to 7ft 7in.

Following his appointment, Lawrence Billinton modified the locomotives through the use of taller chimneys; this saw some

One of 20 Class I1s delivered between September 1906 and December 1907, No 1 was completed at Brighton Works in June 1907. Allocated the BR number 32001, the locomotive was withdrawn in July 1948 before the new number could be applied. The Atlantic was to spend the last four months of its operational career based at Eastbourne, having been reallocated there in March from Tunbridge Wells West.

John Meredith Collection/Online Transport Archive

The fifth of the 10-strong Class I2 to be completed, No 15, emerged from Brighton Works in May 1908. This class was to be regarded as unsuccessful but, unlike the Class I1, was never rebuilt. As a result, withdrawals commenced in 1933 and all had been withdrawn by the end of the decade; two, however, were to find a second life during the Second World War and survived until scrapped in the early 1950s.
Harry Luff Collection/Online Transport Archive

improvement but the major change was to come post-grouping. Between 1923 and 1932 all were rebuilt into Class I1x through the replacement of their original boilers by spare larger ones reused from Class B4 or unsuperheated Class I3s following their rebuilding. As rebuilt, the locomotives performed much better and were to see some success on the Oxted line. Although two of the class — Nos 2597 and 2600 — were withdrawn in December 1946 and October 1944 respectively, the remaining 18 passed to BR in January 1948; however, withdrawal thereafter was rapid with all being taken out of service by the end of July 1951. Only one of the class — No 32005 — was to carry its BR number.

Recognising that there were issues with the original design, Marsh modified it for the production of the I2 class. These were fitted with a longer wheelbase, larger boiler (with a diameter of 4ft 6in rather than 4ft 3in) and modified front end (an extended smokebox on a saddle). A total of 10 were ordered; initially it was planned that five would be fitted with traditional saturated steam boilers produced at Brighton and five with superheated boilers to be supplied by North British. However, delays in the delivery of the latter resulted in all 10 — Nos 11-20 — being fitted with non-superheated boilers. The revised design, however, retained the Achilles' heel of the earlier design: the small firebox. The class was not a success

but operated, without rebuilding, until the 1930s; the first was withdrawn in 1933 and the last succumbed six years later. Two, Nos 2013 and 2037, were not scrapped immediately; placed over the pits at Bournemouth shed they were used, along with sandbags, to create air raid shelters. This was not to be the end of their career, however, as both were transferred, having been relocated to the Eastleigh scrap line in 1941, to the Longmoor Military Railway in 1942 as WD Nos 2400 and 2401 (renumbered 72400/01 in 1944). No 72400 briefly carried the name *Earl Roberts* during 1945 and. The two locomotives were withdrawn in October 1946 and sold to Abelson & Co (Engineers) Ltd of Birmingham two years later. Advertised for sale, the two appeared on shed at Guildford — see the photograph in *Southern Way 65* — in July 1949. Remaining at Guildford until July 1951, the pair was then stored at Godalming Goods before being exported — for scrap probably — to Belgium in February 1952.

Once the delayed superheated boilers arrived from North British they were fitted to a further five of the basic 'I2' design; the new locomotives were designated Class I4. The new locomotives differed from the earlier class in having reduced boiler pressure — from 170lb to 160lb — and increased cylinder diameter (from 17½in to 20in) but retained the small firebox. Whilst superheating on the Class I3 had proved successful, it did not result in a significant improvement in the operation of the 'I2' design. Whilst there were plans to modify them similarly to the 'I1s', these were never progressed and all were withdrawn between January 1936 and May 1940.

The most successful of Marsh's four designs of 4-4-2T was undoubtedly the 'I3'. The first of the class — No 21 — emerged from Brighton Works in October 1907. Effectively a tank version of Robert Billinton's earlier Class B4 4-4-0, the new design incorporated a larger firebox. No 21 was also fitted with 6ft 9in driving wheels; subsequent examples were fitted with 6ft 7½in wheels. A second locomotive — No 22 — was also ordered at the same time; when completed in March 1908, however, this differed from the earlier example in being fitted with a Schmidt superheater, with Marsh having been persuaded to experiment with the modification by the railway's chief draughtsman, B. K. Field. No 21 was equipped with 19in by 26in cylinders with a saturated boiler of 180lb; No 22 had 21in by 26in cylinders along with an extended smokebox carried by a saddle. When completed, No 22 was the first express locomotive to be superheated.

With the two locomotives available, the railway undertook several months of trials; these saw both locomotives perform well but the directors were not initially convinced that the benefits from superheating outweighed the additional costs, although No 22 had shown better fuel consumption and cost of maintenance. A further 10 locomotives were ordered; six of these — Nos 27-30 and 75 and 76 — were fitted with conventional boilers and four — Nos 23-26 — with superheaters. Experience with the additional locomotives confirmed that the superheated model outperformed the saturated version, being capable of hauling the heaviest of LBSCR services. With the experience gained, a further five of the superheated version — Nos 77-81 — were completed under Marsh with a final batch of 10 — Nos 82-91 — being completed under Marsh's successor, Lawson Billinton, in 1912. This later batch of locomotives had a number of detailed differences from the earlier 17. This included being fitted with a second — vacuum — brake and having a higher cab roof.

At the end of the First World War Billinton determined that, as their original boilers became due for replacement, the non-superheated examples would be converted to superheated; however, only one example — No 21 — was so modified prior to the LBSCR's loss of independence in 1923. Post-grouping, Richard Maunsell undertook the conversion of the surviving saturated locomotives using his own design of superheater,

With its builder's plate prominent on the front splasher, No 22 was the second of the 'I3' class to be completed — in March 1908 — and was fitted from new with a Schmid superheater. At the time, the LBSCR was experimenting with superheating its locomotives and No 21 — delivered in October 1907 — lacked superheating. Both performed well but superheating added to the costs and so the next batch to be completed — 10 locomotives — saw four fitted with superheaters and six without. As experience indicated that superheating reduced the costs of operation, subsequent Class I3 locomotives were delivered with superheaters from new with the non-superheated examples being fitted after the First World War. No 22 — as BR No 32022 — survived until May 1951, being based at Tunbridge Wells West throughout the BR era. *John Meredith Collection/Online Transport Archive*

with work being completed between 1925 and 1927.

The 'I3s' were to dominate passenger services on the Brighton main line until they were supplanted by the 'King Arthur' and River classes in the mid-1920s, when they were transferred to secondary lines around Crowborough and Tunbridge Wells. Displaced as the electric network expanded, with modification to reduce the height of the boiler mountings and cab roof, the class was cleared to operate over the South Eastern. In 1938 their area of operation was extended even further with four being relocated to Salisbury on the South Western for use on services to Portsmouth. Even more

unusually, a pair found themselves transferred to Worcester for operation by the GWR between there and Gloucester.

Latterly, however, all of the class returned to service on the South Central. One — No 2024 — was withdrawn as life-expired in November 1944; the remaining 26, however, passed into BR ownership in 1948 although not all were to receive their new BR numbers. All were taken out of service between January 1950 and May 1952.

All of the LBSCR 4-4-2Ts were scrapped.

LBSCR No	New	Later SR No	Date Rebuilt	BR No (allocated)/ Date renumbered	Withdrawn	Notes
Class I1						
1	June 1907	2001	December 1931	(32001)	July 1948	Shorter wheelbase
2	July 1907	2002	May 1931	(32002)	July 1951	Shorter wheelbase
3	July 1907	2003	September 1931	(32003)	July 1948	Shorter wheelbase
4	June 1907	2004	January 1932	(32004)	November 1948	Shorter wheelbase
5	August 1907	2005	August 1931	32005 May 1948	June 1951	Shorter wheelbase
6	September 1907	2006	February 1932	(32006)	September 1948	Shorter wheelbase
7	October 1907	2007	October 1931	(32007)	September 1948	Shorter wheelbase
8	October 1907	2008	February 1931	(32008)	June 1951	Shorter wheelbase
9	November 1907	2009	December 1929	(32009)	April 1951	Shorter wheelbase
10	December 1907	2010	October 1929	(32010)	September 1948	Shorter wheelbase
595	September 1906	2595	January 1927	(32595)	June 1951	
596	November 1906	2596	July 1925	(32596)	June 1951	
597	December 1906	2597	May 1928	N/A	December 1946	
598	January 1907	2598	November 1925	(32598)	September 1948	
599	February 1907	2599	October 1928	(32599)	September 1948	
600	March 1907	2600	May 1927	N/A	October 1944	
601	April 1907	2601	February 1928	(32601)	January 1948	
602	April 1907	2602	December 1926	(32602)	June 1951	
603	June 1907	2603	August 1928	(32603)	April 1951	
604	April 1907	2604	August 1927	(32604)	September 1948	

LBSCR No	New	Later SR No	Date Rebuilt	BR No (allocated)/ Date renumbered	Withdrawn	Notes
Class I2						
11	December 1907	2011		N/A	January 1933	
12	March 1908	2012		N/A	March 1935	
13	April 1908	2013		N/A	January 1939	Became WD 72400 *Earl Roberts*
14	April 1908	2014		N/A	February 1933	
15	May 1908	2015		N/A	January 1936	
16	June 1908	2016		N/A	September 1933	
17	July 1908	2017		N/A	January 1938	
18	July 1908	2018		N/A	April 1936	
19	July 1908	2019		N/A	November 1937	Became WD 72401
20	August 1908	2020		N/A	February 1938	

When completed in September 1906, No 595 was the first of Earle's 4-4-2T designs to be completed. Like all of the I1' class it was rebuilt as an 'I1x'; the locomotive is pictured here post-January 1927 — the month it was converted — still bearing its first Southern Railway number as B595. As rebuilt the Class I1x proved more successful and all bar two passed to BR in 1948; however, apart from No 32005 none received their allocated BR number and all were withdrawn by the end of June 1951. As Southern No 2595, the locomotive was taken out of service from Bricklayers Arms that month. *Peter N. Williams Collection/Online Transport Archive*

An undated view — but pre-January 1949 as it received its BR identity that month — sees 'I3' No 2079 in its final Southern condition. New in November 1910, No 79 was one of the class that was delivered from Brighton Works with a superheater fitted from new. Based at Three Bridges for its entire BR career, No 32079 was withdrawn in early November 1950. *Peter N. Williams/Online Transport Archive*

LBSCR No	New	Later SR No	Date Rebuilt	BR No (allocated)/ Date renumbered	Withdrawn	Notes
Class I3			Date superheated			
21	October 1907	2021	September 1919	32021 1949	September 1951	
22	March 1908	2022	From new	32022 January 1949	May 1951	
23	February 1909	2023	From new	32023 May 1949	July 1951	
24	March 1909	2024	From new	N/A	November 1944	
25	March 1909	2025	From new	(32025)	January 1950	
26	March 1909	2026	From new	32026 October 1949	August 1951	
27	May 1909	2027	February 1925	32027 March 1949	February 1951	
28	December 1909	2028	October 1923	32028 March 1949	September 1951	
29	December 1909	2029	May 1927	32029 January 1949	February 1951	
30	March 1910	2040	January 1926	32030 April 1949	August 1951	
75	March 1910	2075	November 1925	32075 1951	October 1951	
76	March 1910	2076	January 1927	32076 April 1949	December 1950	
77	October 1910	2077	From new	32077 July 1948	March 1951	
78	November 1910	2078	From new	32078 May 1949	January 1951	
79	November 1910	2079	From new	32079 January 1949	November 1951	
80	December 1910	2080	From new	(32080)	March 1950	
81	December 1910	2081	From new	32081 December 1948	August 1951	
82	August 1912	2082	From new	32082 September 1948	June 1951	
83	August 1912	2083	From new	32083 June 1949	June 1951	
84	August 1912	2084	From new	32084 August 1948	March 1951	
85	August 1912	2085	From new	32085 March 1949	July 1950	
86	September 1912	2086	From new	32086 May 1948	October 1951	
87	November 1912	2087	From new	32087 May 1948	October 1950	
88	November 1912	2088	From new	32088 July 1949	October 1950	
89	December 1912	2089	From new	32089 April 1949	April 1951	
90	March 1913	2090	From new	32090 July 1948	November 1950	
91	March 1913	2091	From new	32091 1951	April 1952	Scrapped at Ashford; the first ex-LBSCR express passenger locomotive to be disposed of there

LBSCR No	New	Later SR No	Date Rebuilt	BR No (allocated)/ Date renumbered	Withdrawn	Notes
Class I4						
31	September 1908	2031	From new	N/A	January 1936	
32	November 1908	2032	From new	N/A	July 1937	
33	November 1908	2033	From new	N/A	July 1937	
34	December 1908	2034	From new	N/A	May 1940	
35	January 1939	2035	From new	N/A	February 1937	

	Class I1	Class I1X	Class I2	Class I3	Class I4
Driving wheel	5ft 6in	5ft 6in	5ft 6in	6ft 7½in (6ft 9in – No 21)	5ft 6in
Trailing Wheel	4ft 0in	4ft 0in	4ft 0in	4ft 0in	4ft 0in
Weight	66½ tons	66½ tons	67 tons	73 tons	67 tons
Cylinders	17½in x 26in	17½in x 26in	17½in x 26in	21in x 26in (19in x 26in - No 21)	17½in x 26in
Boiler pressure	170lb	170lb	170lb	180lb	160lb
Water capacity	1,839 gall (595-97) 1,924 gall (598-604, 1-10)	1,839 gall (595-97) 1,924 gall (598-604, 1-10)	2,238 gall	2,110 gall	2,238 gall
Tractive effort	17,430lb	17,430lb	17,430lb	22,065lb	16,400lb

On 22 May 1948, No 2081 — still bearing its Southern number and lettering — is seen approaching East Grinstead (High Level) with a train from Tunbridge Wells. Allocated at the time to Three Bridges shed, the locomotive was renumbered towards the end of the year prior to being transferred to Eastbourne in May 1949. It was to remain on the South Coast for some 18 months prior to returning to Three Bridges in early 1951. It was withdrawn from this shed in early August the same year. *John Meredith/Online Transport Archive*

Opposite top: **Recorded post-January 1949, when it was renumbered by BR, is No 32029. During its BR career the locomotive was to be allocated to three sheds: Tunbridge Wells West until October 1950 and again from early 1951 through to withdrawal at the end of February that year, Eastbourne from October 1950 for a month and then Three Bridges until early 1951.** *J. M. Jarvis/Online Transport Archive*

Bottom: **Pictured on shed at Tunbridge Wells West on 11 July 1950 is 'I3' No 32086. Allocated to Brighton throughout its BR career, the locomotive was officially withdrawn on 6 October 1951 but was noted operational on the 17th. This was, however, very much a swansong as the records indicate that it was being cut up at Eastleigh eight days later.** *J. M. Jarvis/Online Transport Archive*

Proudly bearing its 75A — Brighton — shedplate is No 32091, which is seen here towards the end of its life as it was reallocated to the shed in early 1952; this was to be the last of the '13' class to remain in service and the only one to survive into that year. Only renumbered in 1951 — the last of the class to receive its BR number — No 32091 had previously been allocated to Eastbourne and Three Bridges in BR ownership. Withdrawn in early May 1952, the Atlantic was to be scrapped at Ashford — the first ex-LBSCR express passenger locomotive to be disposed of there — a year later.
Arthur Davenport/Online Transport Archive

The Seaton Branch

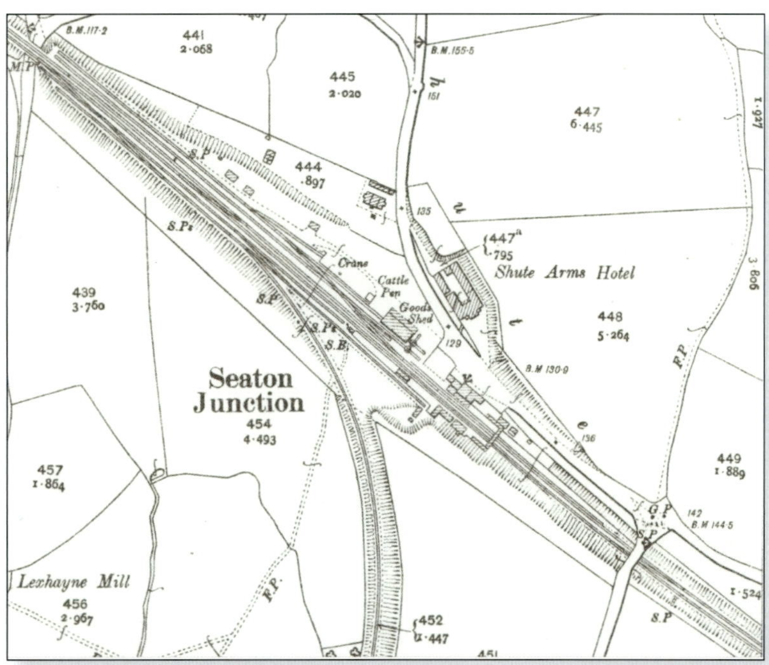

It was not only the Somerset & Dorset that closed officially on 7 March 1966; two other ex-Southern lines succumbed at the same time: the lines from Seaton Junction to Seaton and from Christ's Hospital to Shoreham via Steyning. In addition local services were also withdrawn on the line from Salisbury to Exeter.

A traditional harbour on the south coast of Devon, Seaton, by the middle of the 19th century, had declined in importance; reduced largely to a fishing port, the town benefited from the growth in popularity of seaside holidays. When, however, the LSWR opened its line through to Exeter, the railway bypassed the town; in order to provide a connection to that part of Devon, a station — Colyton for Seaton — was opened with the route on 19 July 1860. With the support of the local population, the Seaton & Beer Railway was authorised by an Act that received its Royal Assent on 13 July 1863. The Act authorised the construction of a 4¼-mile branch from a junction with the LSWR to a station on the east of the town. The new railway's authorised capital was £36,000 with the ability to raise an extra £12,000 by loan if required. Following a meeting on 5 December 1863 the noted engineer William Robert Galbraith was appointed the line's engineer, with Sir Walter Trevelyan made chairman.

On 8 January 1864 a contract was signed with Howard Ashton Holden for the construction of the line. However, progress was not rapid, in April 1865, Holden was threatened by the company with the suspension of his contract; five months later, on 27 September, this threat was carried out and Holden's involvement ceased. The railway struggled to find an alternative contractor and additional funding — through the issue of £12,000 in preference shares and a £4,000 loan — was obtained. Ultimately, Galbraith himself oversaw the completion of the project although the planned opening date in 1867 was missed.

With work completed, Lt-Col William Yolland inspected the line on behalf of the Board of Trade; he made a number of adverse comments about the line and its proposed operation. The most significant of these concerned the proposed operational arrangements at the junction station. Here, the S&BR had proposed that branch trains headed onto the main line for a distance of some 200 yards before being propelled back into the westbound (Down) platform of the main line station; the process being reversed for trains heading towards Seaton. A second inspection by Yolland was held on 19 February 1868; this time all bar one of his minor concerns had been resolved but there remained the major problem of how trains were handled at the

Seaton Junction station and environs in 1903.
Reproduced with the permission of the National Library of Scotland

junction. In a classic case of it's not what you know but who you know, Trevelyan arranged to meet the President of the Board of Trade, Charles Gordon-Lennox, 6th Duke of Richmond, which resulted in an agreement whereby the railway was permitted to open using the contentious means of accessing the station provided that a new platform on the branch line itself was completed within six months of a request made by the Board of Trade.

From the outset it had been expected that the LSWR would undertake the operation of the line although even this arrangement was not without difficulties prior to the branch's opening. Following objections by the larger railway, which were raised in a letter of February 1868 and which were rejected by the S&BR, the issues raised were subject to arbitration. The resulting decisions, conveyed in a letter of 15 March 1868, were largely in favour of the S&BR. With all the major issues now out of the way, it was now possible to open the line. The branch opened throughout on 16 March 1868. There were two intermediate stations — Colyton Town (to differentiate it from the junction station which was renamed Colyton Junction

contemporaneously with the line) and Colyford with services being worked by the LSWR. Colyton Junction was renamed Seaton Junction in July 1869 but it was not until 1890 that Colyton dropped the 'Town' suffix.

As part of the S&BR's original Act, powers were made for the construction of a toll bridge across the Axe to permit residents of Axmouth to reach the railway. In December 1875 work on the bridge was contracted to William Jackson with the work being completed by the civil engineer Philip Brannon. The three-arch structure was opened on 24 April 1877; constructed in concrete (the third to be so completed), the bridge — which is now listed Grade II* — is believed to be the oldest concrete bridge to survive in Britain as the earlier two bridges have subsequently been demolished. When the LSWR took over the S&BR, the new owners had no interest in taking over the bridge and so this, with the rights to claim tolls for its use, passed to Sir A. W. Trevelyan. Although no longer used by motor vehicles, it remains accessible to pedestrians and cyclists.

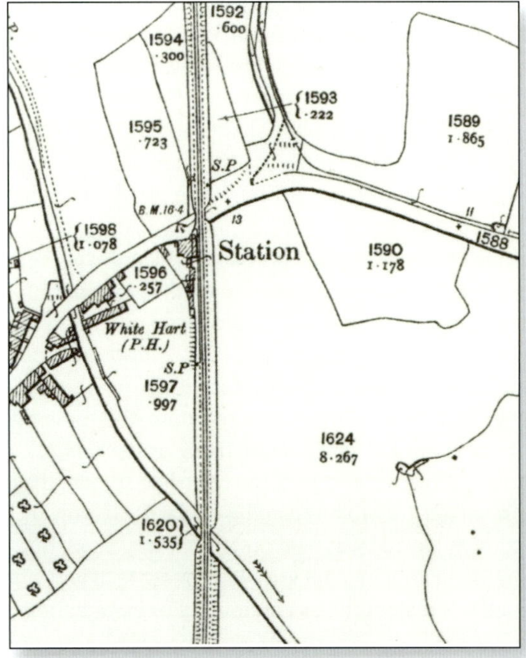

Colyton station and environs in 1903.
Reproduced with the permission of the National Library of Scotland

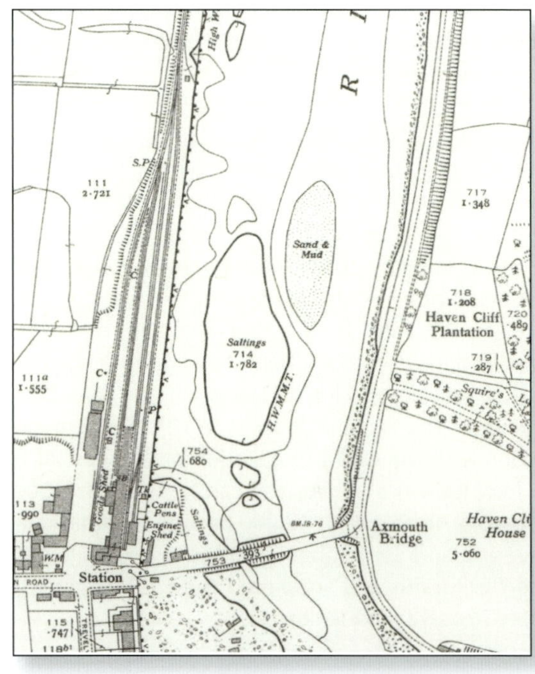

Colyford station and environs in 1903.
Reproduced with the permission of the National Library of Scotland

Seaton station and environs in 1939.
Reproduced with the permission of the National Library of Scotland

SEATON JUNCTION and SEATON.—London and South Western.

Down. — Week Days.

Miles / Station	mrn	mrn	mrn	mrn	mrn	aft	aft	aft	aft
120 London ...... dep	6 10	6 8	8 50	1115	..	1 0	3 30	..	..
123 Exeter (Queen St.) »	6 38	9 15	1027	12 7	1 5	3 25	4 40	6 7	7 40
— Seaton Junction ...... dep	7 55	1015	1115	1 8	3 7	4 22	5 45	7 10	8 40
1¾ Colyton	8 2	1021	1121	1 14	3 14	4 28	5 51	7 16	8 46
2½ Colyford	8 7	1025	1125	1 18	3 19	4 32	5 55	7 20	8 50
4¼ Seaton ...... arr	8 12	1030	1130	1 23	3 24	4 37	6 0	7 25	8 55

Up. — Week Days.

Miles / Station	mrn	mrn	mrn	aft	aft	aft	aft	aft	aft
1¼ Seaton ...... dep	7 5	9 43	1045	1230	2 38	3 52	5 6	6 30	8 10
1¼ Colyford	7 11	9 48	1050	1235	2 43	3 57	5 11	6 35	8 15
2½ Colyton	7 16	9 53	1055	1240	2 48	4 2	5 17	6 40	8 20
4½ Seaton Junc. 120, 123 arr	7 24	10 0	11 2	1247	2 55	4 9	5 25	6 47	8 27
28½ 120 Exeter (Queen St.) arr	8 43	11 4c	1250	1 55	3 41	..	6 23	7 55	1029
152½ 123 London (Waterloo) »	11 31	3 15	4 40	..	8 7	1034	..	3d35	..

c Arrives at 10 50 mrn. on Fridays.   d Via Eastleigh.   o Fridays only.

FRATTON AND SOUTHSEA and EAST SOUTHSEA (Motor Cars—1st and 3rd class).—L. & S. W. and L. B. & S. C.—1¼ miles.
Fratton and Southsea to East Southsea every 20 minutes from 8 mrn. to 7 20 aft., calling at Jessie Road Bridge and Albert Road Bridge.
East Southsea to Fratton and Southsea every 20 minutes from 8 10 mrn. to 7 30 aft., calling at Albert Road Bridge and Jessie Road Bridge.
☞ Cars connect at Fratton with the Principal Trains to and from London, Southampton, Basingstoke, Salisbury, Winchester, Chichester, Arundel, Brighton, &c.

The timetable for the branch as recorded in *Bradshaw* for 1910.

Initially the S&BR retained its independence, but towards the end of the 1870s the company sought to lease the line to either the GWR or the LSWR; in the event, terms were agreed with the latter and, on 1 January 1880, the line was leased to the LSWR for an initial £1,000 per annum. The lease included a clause giving the LSWR an option to purchase the S&BR at a later date. This option was exercised on 1 January 1888 when the life of the S&BR as an independent railway came to an end. Shortly after the LSWR's takeover, in 1880, the platform at Seaton station was extended by 60 yards in order to accommodate the increasing volume of passenger traffic. Initially the line was operated by Beattie 2-2-2WTs; these were

The timetable for services over the line for the period from September 1960 until June 1961.

Table 44 — SEATON JUNCTION and SEATON
(Including Axminster and Seaton by Omnibus on Sundays)

Down — Week Days

Miles / Station	am	..	am	am	..	am	..	pm	pm	C	pm	pm	..	pm	A	pm	pm	pm	pm	..	pm	pm H	..
Seaton Junction dep	8 10	..	8 49	9 46	..	1043	..	12 1	1236	1 5	2 5	2 45	..	3 15	4 47	5 31	6 38	7 5	8 3	..	8 44	H	..
1½ Colyton	8 14	..	8 53	9 50	..	1047	..	12 5	1240	1 9	2 9	2 49	..	3 19	4 51	5 35	6 42	7 9	8 7	..	8 48	10 2	..
2½ Colyford	8 17	..	8 56	9 53	..	1050	..	12 8	1243	1 12	2 12	2 52	..	3 22	4 54	5 38	6 45	7 12	8 10	..	8 51	10 6	..
4¼ Seaton arr	8 20	..	8 59	9 56	..	1053	..	1211	1246	1 15	2 15	2 55	..	3 25	4 57	5 41	6 48	7 15	8 13	..	8 54	1018	..

Up — Week Days

Miles / Station	am	..	am	..	B	..	am	..	pm	C	pm	pm	..	pm	..	pm	pm	..	pm	..	pm	..	..
Seaton dep	7 50	..	8 26	..	10 2	..	1141	..	1216	1250	1 37	2 20	..	3 46	..	5 9	6 10	..	7 41	..	8 18	..	..
1¼ Colyford	7 55	..	8 31	..	10 7	..	1146	..	1221	..	1 42	2 25	..	3 51	..	5 14	6 15	..	7 46	..	8 23	..	..
2¾ Colyton	7 59	..	8 35	..	1011	..	1150	..	1225	..	1 46	2 29	..	3 58	..	5 18	6 19	..	7 50	..	8 27	..	..
4¼ Seaton Junction arr	8 3	..	8 39	..	1015	..	1154	..	1229	1 0	1 50	2 33	..	4 4	..	5 22	6 23	..	7 54	..	8 31	..	..

Sundays — By Southern or Western National Omnibus (Times subject to alteration. See note W)

Station	am	pm	pm	pm	pm	pm	pm	pm	pm	pm	pm	pm
Axminster (Square) dep	1138	1 33	2 29	2†50	3†58	5 0	6† 8	6†35	7 40	8†18	9†49	10 5
Colyton .... „	12 0	1 55	2 51	3 12	4 20	5 22	6 30	6 57	8 2	8 40	1011	1027
Colyford .... „	12 4	1 59	2 55	3 16	4 24	5 26	6 34	7 1	8 6	8 44	1015	1031
Seaton (Front) arr	1211	2 6	3 7	3 28	4 31	5 38	6 41	7 13	8 18	8 51	1022	1038

Station	am	pm	pm	pm	pm	pm	pm	pm	pm	pm	pm	pm
Seaton (Front) dep	9 45	1215	1 20	2 10	3 30	4 35	5 40	6 5	6 25	7 5	8 0	9 25
Colyford .... „	9 52	1222	1 32	2 17	3 42	4 42	5 52	6 12	6 37	7 12	8 12	9 37
Colyton .... „	9 56	1226	1 36	2 21	3 46	4 46	5 56	6 16	6 41	7 16	8 16	9 41
Axminster (Square) arr	1018	1248	1 58	2 43	4 8	5 8	6 18	6 38	7 3	7 38	8 38	10 3

A Through Carriages from Waterloo, dep 1 0 pm (Table 35).   **B** Through Carriages to Waterloo, arr 2 15 pm (Table 35).
C Commences 1st May, 1961   **H** By Southern or Western National Omnibus from **Axminster** Station, dep 9 40 pm, to Seaton (Sea front).   **W** Passengers from or to stations west of Seaton Junction holding Rail tickets from or to Seaton, Colyford, and Colyton routed via Seaton Junction, when using the Omnibus Service, are required to pay the excess rail fare between Axminster and Seaton Junction.   † Axminster Station.

supplanted primarily by Class O2 and T1 0-4-4Ts in the 1890s although the occasional Adams-designed radial 4-4-2Ts were also employed. For the line's first 30 years, it was operated under the 'one engine in steam' principle; it was not until the opening of an intermediate box at Colyton on 5 March 1899 that the Tyers electric tablet system was introduced.

Passing to the SR in 1923, it was over the next two decades that considerable changes were made. Some 60 years after the Board of Trade had accepted the 'temporary' platform arrangements at Seaton Junction, the station was remodelled during 1927 and 1928 with a dedicated platform serving the branch opening on 13 February 1927. Three years later, auto-train operation commenced and, in its later operation by steam (until the Western Region took over), these were hauled by Class M7 0-4-4Ts. Towards the end of the 1930s, the existing layout at Seaton was altered; this required the rebuilding of the small engine shed that served the terminus with the actual station also being rebuilt. This was completed in 1937 in an Art Deco style.

Opposite top: **With dedicated branch brake van No S55703 — lettered 'To work on the Seaton branch only' — at the buffers, WR 0-6-0PT No 6412 arrives with a service from Seaton. Although undated the view must post-date July 1963 fairly recently as that was when the locomotive was reallocated from Ebbw Junction to Exmouth Junction but it is still bearing its 86A (Ebbw Junction) shed plate. No 6412 was reallocated to Yeovil Town in November 1963 and was to end its BR career based at Gloucester Horton Road from August 1964 until withdrawal at the start of November 1964. Preserved on withdrawal, the locomotive was acquired by the Dart Valley Railway and used on the line's reopening special on 5 April 1969. At the time of writing, the 0-6-0PT is undergoing its 10-year overhaul, having been taken out of service at the end of 2024.** *Phil Tatt/Online Transport Archive*

Bottom: **The branch line service stands in the platform at Seaton Junction in Western Region days. Closest to the camera is autotrailer No W243W; this was one of a batch of 10 — Nos W235W to W244W — that was constructed in 1953. These were the last autotrailers built new to a GWR design; the final batch of 12, constructed the same year, were all rebuilt from brake thirds. Two of the batch — Nos W238W and W240W — survive in preservation.** *Phil Tatt/Online Transport Archive*

Colyton station viewed from the north-west. There were limited freight facilities provided at the station but these were withdrawn on 3 February 1964. The station was acquired by the future Seaton Tramway as part of its purchase of the line south to Seaton; however, the agreement allowed the last stationmaster and his family to remain there. This arrangement continued until 1985 when the building was converted into a café and shop. Since then it has been extended as the facilities at the station have been enhanced. *Phil Tatt/Online Transport Archive*

With its single platform and lack of freight facilities, Colyford was the most basic station on the line. It is pictured here looking towards the north and the level crossing with the A3052. Today, Colyford is the location for a passing loop on the Seaton Tramway and the level crossing is still in use for trams as they head northwards to Colyton. *Phil Tatt/Online Transport Archive*

Opposite top: **The WR autotrain is pictured departing from Colyford with a service towards Seaton Junction. Although most of the station was demolished after the line's closure, the concrete gentlemen's lavatory — seen on the platform — remains, albeit no longer in use.**
Phil Tatt/Online Transport Archive

Bottom: **For many years, both prior to and post-nationalisation, the normal passenger service on the branch was provided by Class M7 0-4-4Ts and push-pull stock, as shown by No 30021 pictured at the terminus shortly before the Southern ceded responsibility for the line to the Western. The 'M7' was based at Exmouth Junction for a decade post-nationalisation — between early 1951 and October 1961 — before it was reallocated to Salisbury. Transferred to Tunbridge Wells West for six months between January and July 1953, it was finally withdrawn from Salisbury in mid-March 1964.**
J. Joyce/Online Transport Archive

SEATON STATION

Having brought the service from Seaton Junction, No 6412 is pictured being watered at the terminus. A small engine shed at Seaton was provided when the line opened in 1868, but this was demolished in 1937 when the station layout was modified. The shed visible on the left in this view was constructed that year in concrete with a corrugated asbestos roof. The shed closed on 14 November 1963 and was subsequently demolished. *Phil Tatt/Online Transport Archive*

The branch passed, initially, to the Southern Region of BR on nationalisation but was transferred to Western control in 1963; this resulted in the last period of steam running being operated by ex-GWR 0-6-0PTs with auto-trailers. This ceased on 4 November 1963 when DMUs took over operation of the line. However, by that date, the future of the branch was already under threat. Listed for closure in the Beeching report, the line lost its freight traffic on 3 February 1964 when the goods yards at Seaton and Colyton were closed. Passenger services were officially withdrawn on 7 March 1966; Seaton Junction station closed at the same time.

This might have been the end of the story; however, revival of part of the line was to come through an unusual route. A company — Modern Electric Tramways Ltd — had operated a number of miniature tramways from the late 1940s onwards;

these had resulted in the creation of a 2ft 0in gauge line that served the sea front at Eastbourne. However, by the mid-1960s it became apparent that the lease under which the tramway was operated would not be renewed. The company, therefore, sought an alternative location. Following the closure of the Seaton branch, the company acquired the line with a view to converting it into a narrow-gauge electric tramway. With the line purchased, a Light Railway Order was obtained in December 1969. The first — short — section of the 2ft 9in gauge line, initially battery operated, opened on 28 August 1970. Over the next decade the line was progressively extended into the town centre at Seaton and along the trackbed northwards to Colyford. The tramway now extends over some three miles with some 12 trams in the passenger fleet housed in a depot built on the site of the demolished station.

Opposite: **The exterior of the station at Seaton; this was rebuilt in the late 1930s. After closure, the station was demolished and the site was subsequently used for the construction of the Seaton Tramway's depot.** *Phil Tatt/Online Transport Archive*

In late February and early March 1965, the LCGB organised its two 'East Devon' tours to traverse the threatened branch lines in the area to the east of Exeter; amongst the routes visited was that to Seaton with Standard 2-6-4T No 80041 employed on both occasions to haul the special to and from Seaton. Here, on the first of the two dates, 28 February, the locomotive is pictured at the terminus prior to running round the stock.
Phil Tatt/Online Transport Archive

Opposite top: **On 20 June 1971 work in progress converting the line to 2ft 9in gauge is viewed from the upper deck of tram No 2.**
Geoffrey Tribe/Online Transport Archive

Bottom: **Pictured at the terminus in Seaton on 15 June 2003 is No 17; this crossbench tram was originally completed in 1988 and was probably Britain's first disabled access tram as some of its seats were removable to permit wheelchairs to be accommodated. The tram was rebuilt as fully-enclosed in 2016 — when the disabled facility was lost (although accommodation was now provided by other trams) — when the tram was renumbered 15.**
Geoffrey Tribe/Online Transport Archive

Class 508 EMUs

The late 1960s saw initial plans developed for a new fleet of EMUs; there were two pressing needs: equipment for planned electrification projects and replacement units for the increasingly aged suburban stock used on the Southern's suburban network. In furtherance of this work, the Railway Technical Centre at Derby constructed a mock-up of the proposed new design; this demonstrated the basic concept of the new rolling stock although the front end was modified before construction work on any new rolling stock was undertaken. In 1970 the decision was taken to produce three experimental units — one two-car and two four-car sets — that would be radically different to those supplied earlier.

Amongst the features of these new units were the adoption of the Scharfenberg automatic coupling, the use of air-operated doors for passenger use, the lack of buffers, fluorescent lighting and the fact that no separate accommodation was provided for the guard. The new units also included new power and control equipment as well as rheostatic braking alongside the more usual electro-pneumatic brakes. The first of the new units — No 4001 (designated Class 4PEP [TOPS Code Class 445] by the Southern) where the 'PEP' stood for Prototype Electro Pneumatic — was delivered from York Works in May 1971; the second unit — No 4002 — was delivered by the end of the same year, with the two-car unit — No 2001 (Class 2PEP [Class 446]) — following in 1972. Whilst the two '4PEPs' were delivered in all-over Rail Blue, No 2001 emerged in unpainted aluminium with red insignia.

The Class 508 units followed on from the prototype Classes 2PEP and 4PEP units that were constructed by BREL at York in 1971. Two of the latter — Nos 4001 and 4002 — were constructed and, like Class 2PEP 2001, were initially based at Wimbledon Park and Strawberry Hill for use on the South Western. Extensive testing was undertaken before the three units entered public service in June 1973. Here No 4001 is seen on test at Raynes Park during the summer of 1971. *Harry Luff/Online Transport Archive*

Following their introduction to passenger service in the early summer of 1973, the prototype stock was used on services to Chessington South, Hampton Court and Shepperton. Here No 4002 leads No 4001 into Clapham Junction with a Down train shortly after their introduction to passenger service. In August 1973 all three units were transferred to the South Eastern but, as a result of a series of failures and incompatibility with other rolling stock, all three were returned to the South Western after a month. The three units were not to remain operational in public service for long, being transferred to departmental stock for the remainder of their lives. All were scrapped between 1987 and 1990. *Harry Luff/Online Transport Archive*

Following testing (which saw the units reformed for evaluation purposes, including the permanent transfer of one of the aluminium cars from No 2001 to a four-car set), the new units, which were based at Strawberry Hill and Wimbledon Park, were put into operation on the lines from Waterloo to Shepperton, Chessington South and Hampton Court; except for a brief period in 1973, when they were tested on suburban lines out of Cannon Street and Charing Cross to Bromley North and Dartford, the trio spent their operational life on the South Western. The first use of the stock in passenger service occurred on 5 June 1973 when an eight-car formation was used to form the 10.56 and 14.26 services from Waterloo to Hampton Court and the 11.43 and 15.13 return workings.

No 2001, reclassified as Class 920 and renumbered 920001, was taken out of passenger service in 1974 and converted into a three-car set (Class 3PEP) through the addition of a new-build trailer coach; this was to facilitate the development of the Class 313 sets for use on the Great Northern suburban lines that required both AC and DC operation. It was also used as a test-bed for the development of the Class 314 units for use on Scottish Region services around Glasgow. Nos 4001 and 4002 remained in passenger service until October 1976 when both were transferred to departmental stock. Reclassified Class 935,

the two units were renumbered 056 and 057. The former, which saw little use on the Southern, being stored at Wimbledon Park, was transferred to the RTC in June 1980. All three of the 'PEP' units were out of use by the mid-1980s; No 056 was scrapped in 1986, No 920001 in 1987 and No 057 in 1990. Alongside the produced Class 313, 314, 315, 507 and 508, the proposed Class 316 units for the planned Picc-Vic link in Manchester would also have been based around the 'PEP' design.

Class 2PEP/4PEP formations in passenger service

Unit No	DMSO	MSO	MSO	DMSO
2001	64300	N/A	N/A	64305
4001	64301	62427	62428	64302
4002	64303	64626	62429	64304

Whilst batches of EMU based around the 'PEP' design were supplied to the Eastern, London Midland and Scottish regions, it was not until 1979 that the Holgate Road, York, Works delivered the 43-strong Class 508 units to the Southern. Unlike the 'PEP' design, which had two+two seating, the '508's had two+three; this meant that the driving vehicles could

In the spring of 1980, No 508016 has just arrived with a Down service at Hampton Court. This was one of the class that returned to the erstwhile Southern Region when it was transferred to Connex and renumbered 508207. Remaining in service until the final demise of the class in December 2008, two of the unit's coaches — Nos 64664 and 64707 — are amongst the handful of survivors from the class, having been converted for use as barrier vehicles.
Harry Luff/Online Transport Archive

accommodate 74 seated passengers whilst intermediate trailers could seat 84. More significantly, whilst every axle of the 'PEP' design was powered, only the four axles on each of the driving vehicles was powered. A total of eight 110hp GEC-built electric motors were fitted. Another difference was that the type was fitted with Tightlock automatic coupling; this enabled the units to be coupled and uncoupled from the driver's cab.

Amongst the electronic and control equipment fitted was a wheel slip/slide protection system. Whilst in theory a useful addition, in practice it proved problematic, with brakes being released inappropriately as a result of a minor slip, thus causing the train to run through stations and pass signals. There were also issues of acceleration when starting away on wet or slippery rails. This led to considerable testing, handled by the region's R&D section at Strawberry Hill, with various modifications tried out. Ultimately a wheel slide protection button was added to the driver's desk which, when applied, overrode the protection system. No 508002 was used for much

of the testing work from Strawberry Hill and was not finally released to passenger service until the end of 1982.

With the units being delivered, testing occurred on the line to Shepperton and on the main line to Basingstoke with driver training also being undertaken. On 17 December 1979 the first revenue-earning service was run; the first service, operated by Nos 508009 and 508008, was the 10.04 from Waterloo to Shepperton. Fleet operation commenced during the spring of 1980. Initial services covered the Waterloo to Chessington, Hampton Court and Shepperton lines as well as the Kingston Loop but as more units were delivered and lines approved, this area was extended. It was whilst working on the South Western that the first serious incident to affect the class occurred; on 21 April 1982 No 508031, forming the 06.34 service from Waterloo, crashed through the buffers at Shepperton and ended up blocking the crossroads alongside Ian Allan Ltd's Terminal House offices. The cause of the accident was found to be faulty braking on the unit.

On 13 November 1982 No 508007 is seen approaching Clapham Junction with the 10.16 service from Waterloo to Shepperton. By this date, operation of the class on the South Western was drawing to a close with the first use in public service on Merseyside having taken place earlier the same year. No 508007 was another of the class to return to the Southern; as No 508204 it survived as Connex No 508204 until December 2008.
Bernard Harrison/Bob Bridger Collection/Online Transport Archive

The beginning of the end for the class on the South Western occurred in November 1981 when Nos 508042 and 508043 were converted to three-car sets and moved to Merseyside; a further three — Nos 508039-41 — followed in February 1983. With the delivery of the Class 455s, all of the Class 508 stock, reduced to three-car rakes, was transferred northwards to replace the older LMS-designed Class 503 stock.

On Merseyside, driver training commenced on 17 February 1982 and initial public operation on the line to Southport began the following month; operation of the class on the Wirral started on 8 June 1984. At privatisation, ownership of the units passed to Angel Trains with the initial lease being held by Merseyrail. The type was to survive in service on Merseyside for some four decades although the operational number had been reduced to 27 by 2010, with three having been transferred to Silverlink and 12 to Southeastern as well as one — No 508118 — withdrawn. All 27 of the surviving Merseyrail units were refurbished by Alstom at Eastleigh between 2002 and 2004. With the introduction of the Class 777 units from 2023 onwards, the Merseyrail Class 508s were gradually withdrawn. A farewell special, operated by Nos 508139 and 508141, ran on 29 October 2023 with the last unit being taken out of service on 16 January 2024. All have subsequently been scrapped.

The first of the units to return to the London area saw 12 that were surplus to requirements on Merseyside leased to Connex South Eastern. This franchisee saw the stored stock as an opportunity to accelerate the process of replacing slam-door stock — Classes 4CEP and 3CEP — on its suburban services. In January 1998 the 12 units were moved from store to Eastleigh Depot where they were refurbished by Wessex Traincare. The first of the units were delivered to Gillingham during March 1998 and, following driver training, the first of the sets re-entered service on 3 August 1998.

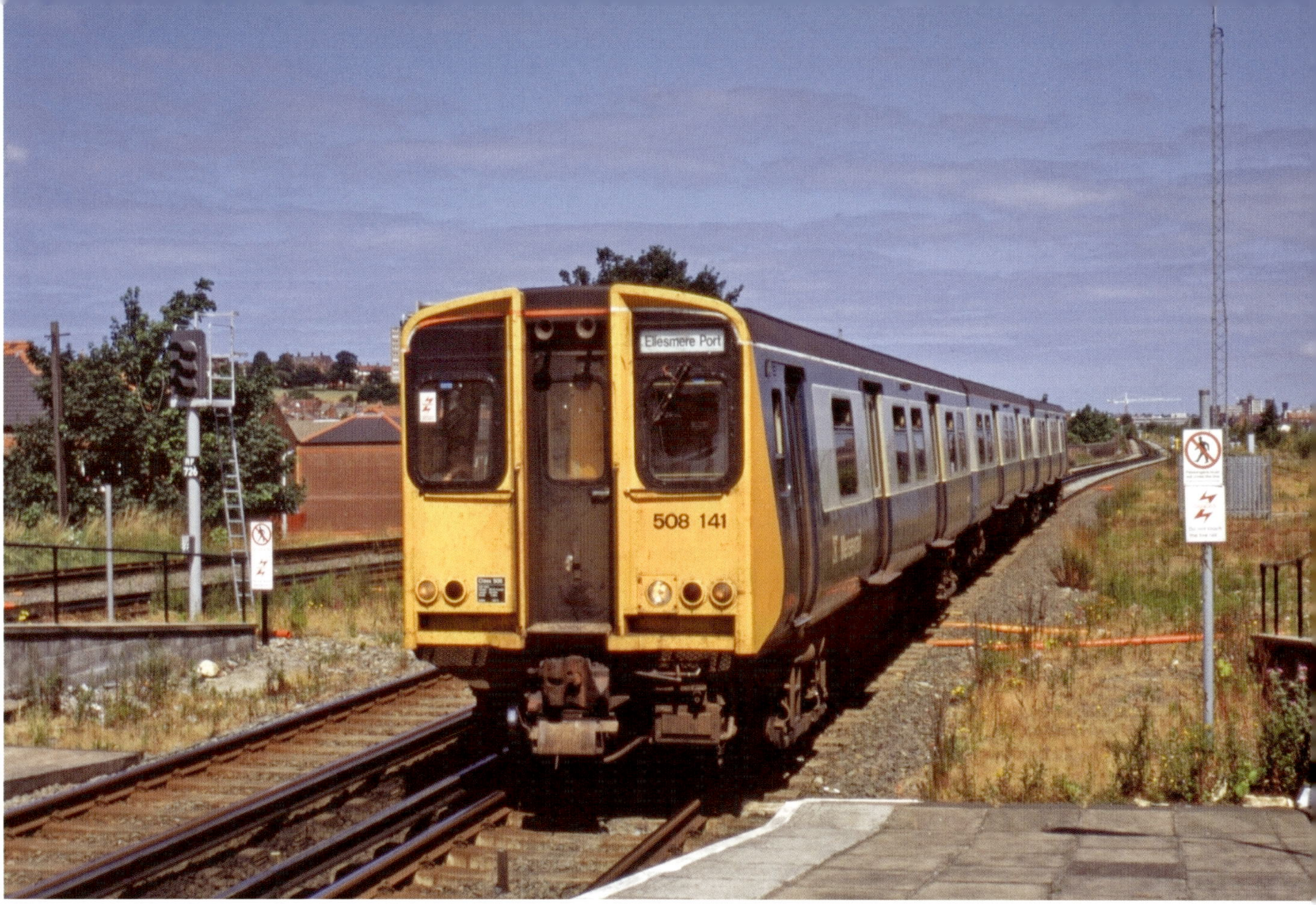
Ellesmere Port
508 141

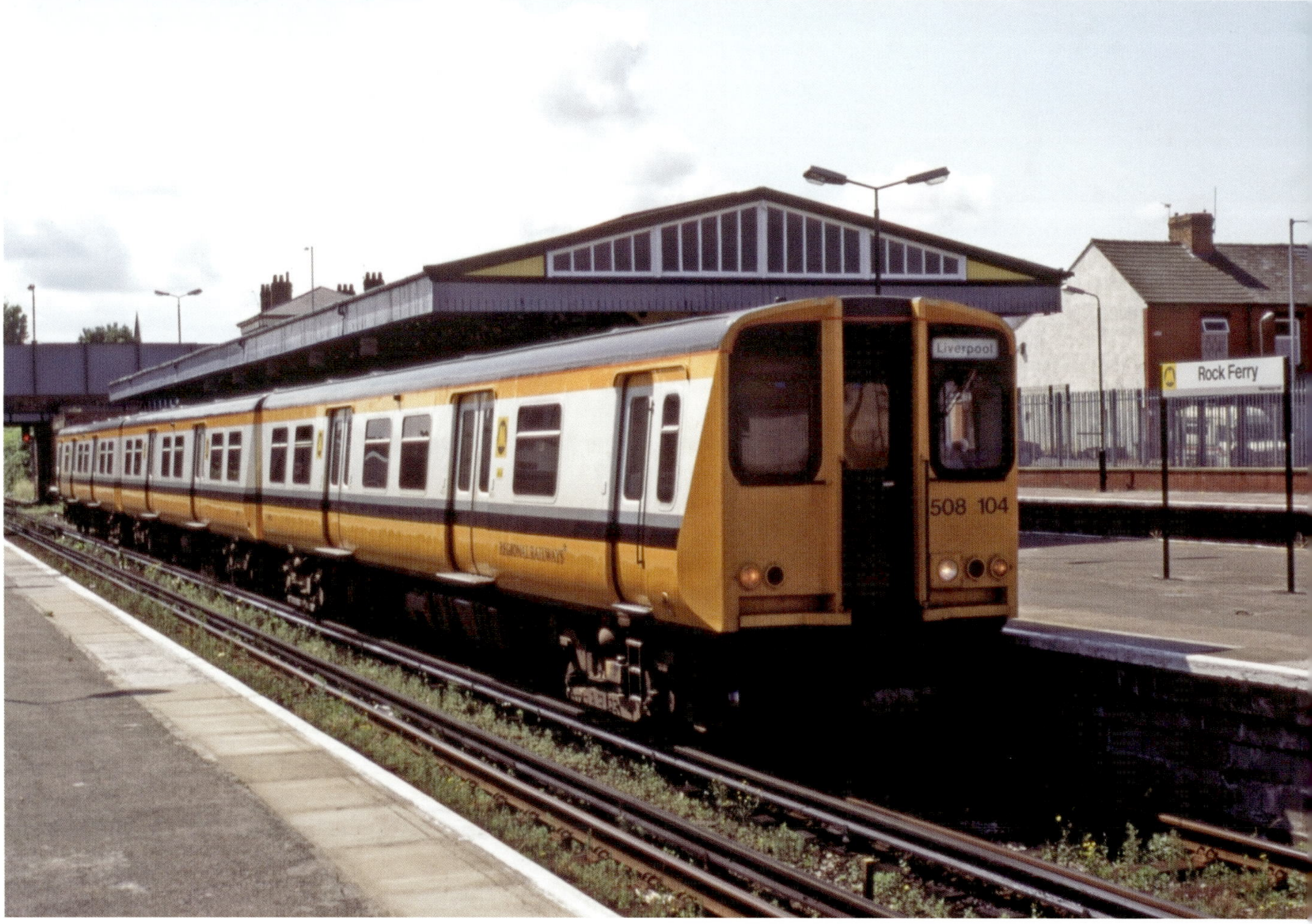
Liverpool
508 104
Rock Ferry

By the end of the 1990s, operational requirements for the class on Merseyside had declined; 12 of the class were transferred to Connex South Eastern in 1996 and others were withdrawn in the early years of the following decade. Pictured stored off lease at New Brighton on 27 June 2002 are Nos 508131 and 508122. Whilst three of the surplus units were transferred to Silverlink at this time, neither of these two units were to return to service and were scrapped. *John/Ray Wood/Online Transport Archive*

The 12 units were initially to be found on services from London Bridge to either Maidstone West or Tunbridge Wells, from Maidstone West to Three Bridges or Strood, Sittingbourne to Sheerness-on-Sea and from Strood to Paddock Wood. On 18 January 2004 both Strood and Higham tunnels were closed temporarily to permit strengthening work to be undertaken; this resulted in the class also being employed on a shuttle working between Gillingham and Strood. The two tunnels were reopened on 18 January 2005.

By this date, Connex South Eastern had ceased to operate its franchise; in June 2003, the Strategic Rail Authority stripped the company of its franchise as a result of poor financial management — the franchisee had already been bailed out by a £58 million injection from the SRA — and a temporary operator, South Eastern Trains (a subsidiary of the SRA), commenced operations on 9 November 2003. The new operator continued until the franchise was re-let to Southeastern (the trading name of London & South Eastern Railway Ltd) which took over on 1 April 2006.

Under South Eastern Trains one of the class again underwent some refurbishment work but the others received no attention. The type's workload was gradually reduced as the delivery of the new Class 376s permitted the older Class 465 'Networker' units to be cascaded to replace some of the Class 508 duties. However, all 12 survived to pass to Southeastern in 2006. The new franchisee immediately announced that a quarter of the fleet was to be withdrawn imminently with the remainder due to depart by the end of the following year. In the event, however, this policy was altered in August 2006. It was decided to retain six of the units, which were overhauled by Wabtec at Doncaster (the first to be so treated being No 508205, which was sent north on 1 June 2007), with the remaining six being taken out of service; five were stored at Chart Leacon with the sixth being used as a source of spare parts. Despite being refurbished relatively recently, the remaining six units were all taken out of service in December 2008 when the London to Tonbridge via Redhill service was transferred from Southeastern to Southern. The units remained in store at various Southeastern depots until all were transferred to Eastleigh for disposal, the majority being scrapped during 2013.

Opposite top: **When the class headed to Merseyside, the units initially retained their blue and grey livery as carried here by No 508141 pictured approaching Rock Ferry on 22 July 1994 with the 11.17 service from Moorfields to Ellesmere Port. This unit — along with No 508139 — operated a farewell tour for the class on 29 October 2023.** *Bernard Harrison/Bob Bridger Collection/Online Transport Archive*

Bottom: **With the sectorisation of BR, new liveries were adopted and, for the Class 508 units, the revised colour scheme — with Regional Railways branding — was predominantly yellow and white as portrayed here by No 508104 at Rock Ferry on 22 July 1994 forming the 11.00 service from Ellesmere Port to Liverpool. This particular unit was one of three that were to survive in service into 2024, all being withdrawn during January that year — the last of the class in public service.** *Bernard Harrison/Bob Bridger Collection/Online Transport Archive*

In order to extend the life of the units that it was retaining, Merseyrail undertook the refurbishment of its units at Eastleigh. Pictured awaiting its turn in the works is No 71505 from unit No 508123 on 23 July 2004. *John/Ray Wood/Online Transport Archive*

One of the refurbished units, No 508110, is pictured here approaching Sandhills with the 11.56 service to Kirby on 23 August 2003. *John/ Ray Wood/Online Transport Archive*

The next of the class to be transferred back were three that were leased to Silverlink in 2003 to supplement the operator's existing fleet of Class 313 units on the DC services to Watford. Before they could commence operation, the trio underwent slight modification to make them compatible with the '313s'. The three units were to survive a decade on this service until replacement by the new Class 378s, the first of which entered service on 29 July 2009. Like the units that had passed to Southeastern, the three sets that were operated by Silverlink spent some time in store before heading to Eastleigh for disposal.

Of the stock, a handful survive: DMSO No 64649, from the first of the class, is preserved on the East Kent Railway; DMSO No 64664 and BDMSO No 64707 have been converted into barrier wagons; the cab of DMSO No 64680 is preserved; BDMSO No 64712 was sold for non-railway use to a farm; and the three coaches from No 508212 (Nos 64681, 71515 and 64724) are in use for training at the Fire Station College at Moreton-in-Marsh.

No/Renumbered					TSO to Class 455	Withdrawn
508001/508101	64649	71483	71526	64692	71526 to (45)5723	To Connex South Eastern
508002/508102	64650	71484	71527	64693	71527 to (45)5728	To Silverlink
508003/508103	64651	71485	71528	64694	61528 to (45)5717	December 2023
508004/508104	64652	71486	71529	64695	71529 to (45)5738	January 2024
508005/508105	64653	71487	71530	64696	71530 to (45)5740	To Connex South Eastern
508006/508106	64654	71488	71531	64697	71531 to (45)5734	To Connex South Eastern
508007/508107	64655	71489	71532	64698	71532 to (45)5709	To Connex South Eastern
508008/508108	64656	71490	71533	64699	71533 to (45)5722	January 2024
508009/508109	64657	71491	71534	64700	71534 to (45)5706	To Connex South Eastern
508010/508110	64658	71492	71535	64701	71535 to (45)5715	August 2020
508011/508111	64659	71493	71536	64702	71536 to (45)5707	October 2023
508012/508112	64660	71494	71537	64703	71537 to (45)5739	November 2023
508013/508113	64661	71495	71538	64704	71538 to (45)5750	To Connex South Eastern
508014/508114	64662	71496	71539	64705	71539 to (45)5714	January 2024
508015/508115	64663	71497	71540	64706	71540 to (45)5703	July 2023
508016/508226	64664	71498	71541	64707	71541 to (45)5725	To Connex South Eastern
508017/508117	64665	71499	71542	64708	71542 to (45)5711	October 2023
508018/508118	64666	71500	71543	64709	71543 to (45)5742	April 2001 following arson attack
508019/508119	64667	71501	71544	64710	71544 to (45)5737	To Connex South Eastern
508020/508120	64668	71502	71545	64711	71545 to (45)5701	December 2023
508021/508121	64669	71503	71546	64712	71546 to (45)5712	To Connex South Eastern
508022/508122	65670	71504	71547	64713	71547 to (45)5702	March 2023
508023/508123	64671	71505	71548	64714	71548 to (45)5704	February 2023
508024/508124	64672	71506	71549	64715	71549 to (45)5733	October 2023
508025/508125	64673	71507	71550	64716	71550 to (45)5729	October 2023
508026/508126	64674	71508	71551	64717	71551 to (45)5730	September 2023
508027/508127	64675	71509	71552	64718	71552 to (45)5732	August 2023
508028/508128	64676	71510	71553	64719	71553 to (45)5721	October 2023
508029/508129	64677	71511	71554	64720	71554 to (45)5736	To Connex South Eastern
508030/508130	64678	71512	71555	64721	71555 to (45)531	October 2023
508031/508131	64679	71513	71556	64722	71556 to (45)5726	December 2023
508032/508132	64680	71514	71557	64723	71557 to (45)5718	To Connex South Eastern
508033/508133	64681	71514	71558	64724	71558 to (45)5719	To Connex South Eastern
508034/508134	64682	71516	71559	64725	71559 to (45)5741	January 2020
508035/508135	64683	71517	71560	64726	71560 to (45)5708	To Silverlink
508036/508136	64684	71518	71561	64727	71561 to (45)524	December 2023
508037/508137	64685	71519	71562	64728	71562 to (45)5727	November 2023
508038/508138	64686	71520	71563	64729	71563 to (45)5735	August 2023
508039/508139	64687	71521	71564	64730	71564 to (45)5716	November 2023
508040/508140	64688	71522	71565	64731	71565 to (45)5705	October 2022
508041/508141	64689	71553	71566	64732	71556 to (45)5710	November 2023
508042/508142	64690	71554	71567	64733	71567 to (45)5713	To Silverlink
508043/508143	64691	71525	71568	64734	71568 to (45)5720	September 2022

Connex sets

Original No	Merseyrail No	Connex No	Withdrawn	Notes
508001	508101	508201	December 2006	Renumbered August 1998; 46459 preserved on East Kent Railway
508005	508105	508202	December 2006	Renumbered April 1998
508006	508106	508203	December 2008	Renumbered June 1998
508007	508107	508204	December 2008	Renumbered May 1998
508009	508109	508205	December 2006	Renumbered July 1998
508013	508113	508206	December 2006	Renumbered August 1998
508016	508116	508207	December 2008	Renumbered June 1998; 64664 and 64707 in use as barrier vehicles
508019	508119	508208	December 2008	Renumbered July 1998
508021	508121	508209	December 2006	Renumbered May 1998; 64712 sold for non-railway use a Rye Farm, Wishaw
508029	508129	508210	December 2008	Renumbered September 1998
508032	508132	508211	December 2008	Renumbered May 1998; Cab of 64680 preserved
508033	508133	508212	December 2008	Renumbered April 1998; 64681, 71515 and 64724 in use at Fire Service College in Moreton-in-Marsh

Silverlink sets

Original No	Silverlink No		Withdrawn	Notes
508002	508301	December 2002	2009	
808035	508302	April 2003	2009	
508041	508303	March 2003	2009	

Bearing its Connex South Eastern livery, No 508209 is pictured forming a service from Sheerness-on-Sea to Sittingbourne at Queenborough on 6 August 1998 This was one of the units withdrawn in December 2006. *Alex Dasi-Sutton*

Connex South Eastern lost its franchise in June 2003 when South Eastern Trains took over operations on a temporary basis until the franchise was relet in April 2006. Pictured at Norwood Junction in Southeastern livery is No 508201 on the 08.33 service from Tonbridge to London Bridge. This is another of the six units withdrawn by the end of 2006. *Alex Dasi-Sutton*

The final iteration of the livery worn by the surviving units transferred to serve Connex South Eastern and its successors was that of Southeastern; here No 508207 is seen on the 13.03 service from London Bridge to Tunbridge Wells at Redhill on 4 October 2008. This was one of the units that remained operational until the final withdrawal of the type in south-east England in December 2008. After withdrawal, the two driver coaches — Nos 64664 and 64707 — were converted for use as barrier vehicles. *Alex Dasi-Sutton*

In 2003 Silverlink leased three of the class to supplement its existing Class 313s on the service to Watford Junction. Prior to use, the three units were slightly modified. On 13 July 2003 No 508302 is pictured at Watford Junction in its newly acquired Silverlink livery. This unit had originally been No 508035. With the transfer of the Watford service to London Overground in November 2007, the existing livery was retained on the three Class 508 units but with London Overground branding. The three units were replaced by new Class 378s in 2010 and stored at Eastleigh for a number of years before being scrapped there in 2013. *Geoffrey Tribe/Online Transport Archive*

SOUTHERN STATIONS 7
SUSSEX EAST

Paul Smith

PLEASE NOTE THAT THE SCALES OF THE MAPS VARY AND ARE FOR ILLUSTRATIVE PURPOSES

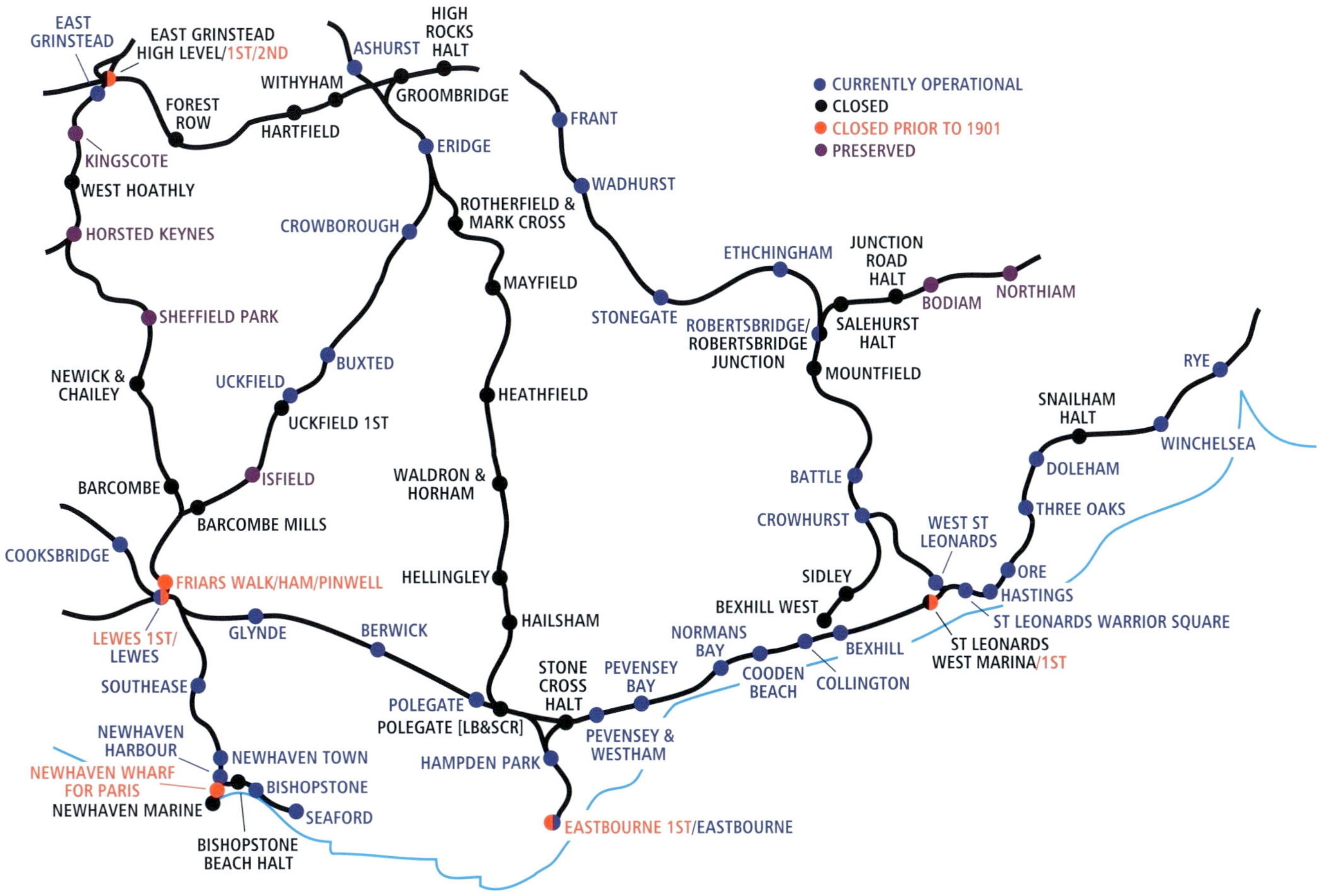

ASHURST

Opened 1 October 1888 by the LB&SCR.

TQ50722 38785

Viewed on 24 June 2017

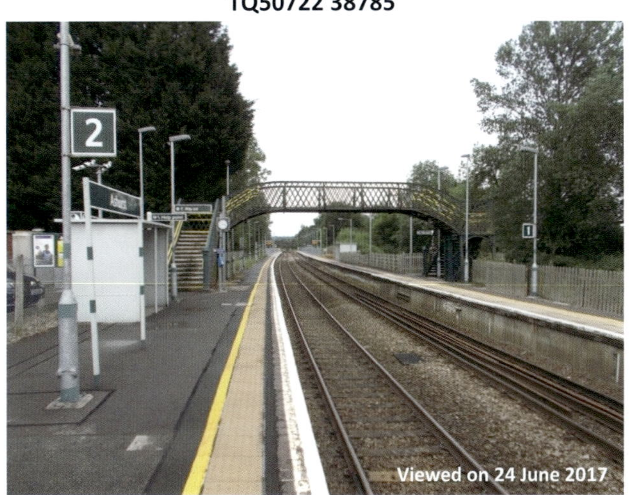

BARCOMBE

Opened 1 August 1882 by the Lewes & East Grinstead Railway as *New Barcombe*, renamed as *Barcombe* 1 January 1885 and closed 30 May 1955 by BR.

Line lifted - Station building and platform in private use

TQ41727 15704

SUSSEX 50.14 (1909)

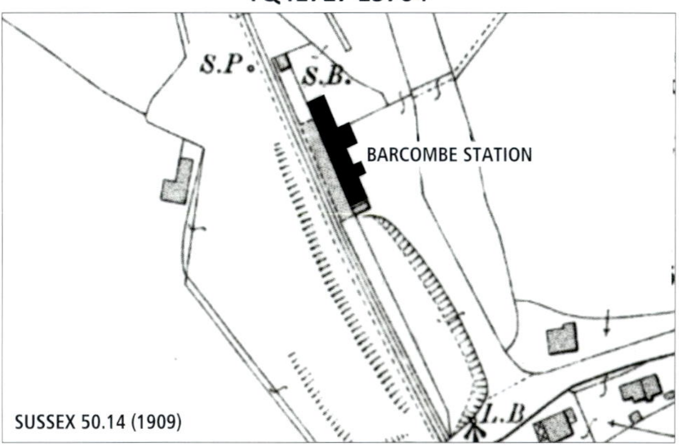

BARCOMBE MILLS

Opened 18 October 1858 by the Lewes & Uckfield Railway as *Barcombe*, renamed as *Barcombe Mills* 1 January 1885 by the LB&SCR and closed 4 May 1969 by BR.
Line lifted - Station building and platform in private use as a restaurant with holiday chalets sited on platforms
TQ42961 14926

BATTLE

Opened 1 January 1852 by the SER, closed 8 March 1855 and reopened 30 June 1855.
TQ75481 15552

BERWICK

Opened 27 June 1846 by the London & Brighton Railway as *Berwick*, renamed as *Berwick Sussex* 12 May 1980 by BR and reverted to *Berwick* 11 May 1987.
TQ52543 06820

BEXHILL

Opened 27 June 1846 by the London & Brighton Railway as *Bexhill*, renamed as *Bexhill Central* 9 July 1923 by the SR and reverted to *Bexhill* c1970 by BR.
TQ74369 07517

BEXHILL WEST

Opened 1 June 1902 by the Crowhurst, Sidley & Bexhill Railway as *Bexhill*, closed 1 January 1917 by the SE&CR, reopened 1 March 1919, renamed as *Bexhill-on-Sea* in 1920, as *Bexhill* 9 July 1923 by the SR, as *Bexhill West* in November 1929 and closed 15 June 1964 by BR.
Line lifted - Platforms demolished - Grade II listed station building in commercial use **TQ73562 07493**

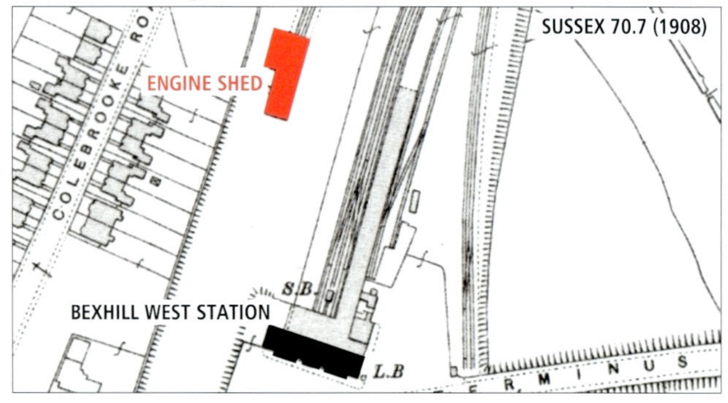

BISHOPSTONE

Opened 26 September 1938 by the SR as *Bishopstone Halt* and renamed as *Bishopstone* 5 May 1969 by BR.
TV46925 99891

BISHOPSTONE BEACH HALT

Opened 1 June 1864 by the LB&SCR as *Bishopstone*, renamed as *Bishopstone Halt* 1 August 1922, closed 26 September 1938 by the SR, reopened 6 April 1939 as *Bishopstone Beach Halt* and finally closed 1 January 1942. *Line Operational – Demolished - Platforms partially extant*

TQ46096 00392

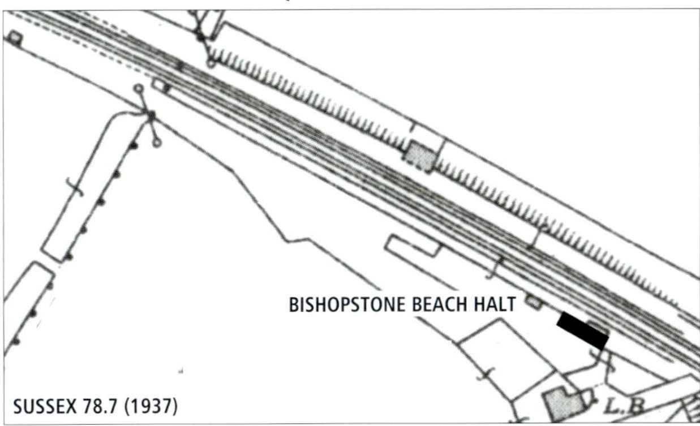

BODIAM

Opened 2 April 1900 by the Rother Valley Light Railway, closed 4 January 1954 by BR and reopened 2 April 2000 by the Kent & East Sussex Railway Preservation Society.

TQ78308 25000

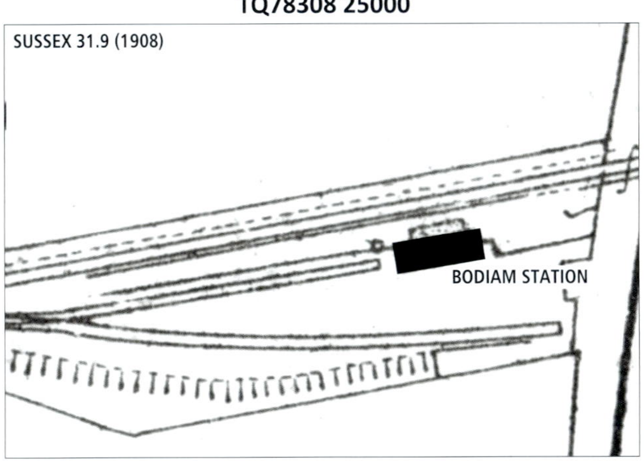

BUXTED

Opened 3 August 1868 by the Brighton, Uckfield & Tunbridge Wells Railway.

TQ49686 23376

COLLINGTON

Opened 11 September 1905 by the LB&SCR as *Collington Wood Halt*, closed 1 September 1906, reopened in June 1911 as *West Bexhill Halt*, renamed as *Collington Halt* 1 November 1929 by the SR and as *Collington* 5 May 1969 by BR.

TQ73089 07291

COODEN BEACH

Opened 11 September 1905 by the LB&SCR as *Cooden Golf Club Halt*, renamed as *Cooden Halt*, as *Cooden Beach Halt* in 1910 and as *Cooden Beach* 7 July 1935 by the SR.

TQ70979 06565

COOKSBRIDGE

Opened cJune 1848 by the LB&SCR as *Cooks Bridge* and renamed as *Cooksbridge* in 1885.

TQ40046 13503

CROWBOROUGH

Opened 3 August 1868 by the Brighton, Uckfield & Tunbridge Wells Railway as *Rotherfield*, renamed as *Crowborough* 1 August 1880 by the LB&SCR, as *Crowborough & Jarvis Brook* 1 May 1897 and reverted to *Crowborough* 12 May 1980 by BR.

TQ53494 29728

CROWHURST

Opened 1 June 1902 by the SE&CR.

TQ76037 12889

DOLEHAM

Opened 1 June 1907 by the SE&CR as *Guestling Halt*, renamed as *Doleham Halt* in 1908 and renamed as *Doleham* 5 May 1969 by BR.

TQ83554 16482

EASTBOURNE (1st)

Opened 15 May 1849 by the LB&SCR and closed in 1866. *Line lifted – Demolished – Station site occupied by housing in Wharf Road*

TV60860 99208 (a)

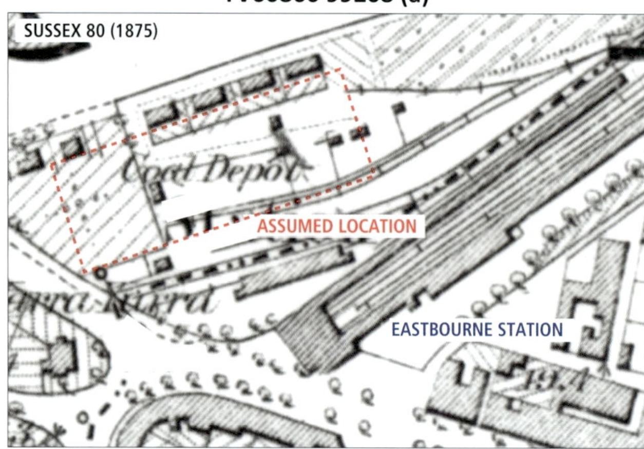

EASTBOURNE

Opened in 1866 by the LB&SCR.

TV61022 99174

EAST GRINSTEAD

Opened 1 August 1882 by the LB&SCR as *East Grinstead Low Level* and renamed as *East Grinstead* by BR.

TQ38793 38198

EAST GRINSTEAD HIGH LEVEL

Opened 15 October 1883 by the LB&SCR and closed 2 January 1967 by BR.

Line lifted – Demolished **TQ38828 38272**

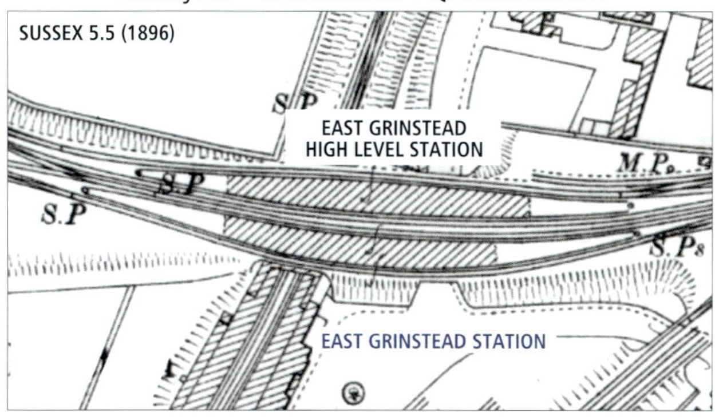

EAST GRINSTEAD (1st)

Opened 9 July 1855 by the East Grinstead Railway and closed 1 October 1866 by the LB&SCR.

Line lifted – Demolished – Station building in commercial use – Beeching Way passes through the station site **TQ39166 38281**

EAST GRINSTEAD (2nd)

Opened 1 October 1866 by the LB&SCR and closed 15 October 1883.

Line lifted – Demolished – Beeching Way passes through the station site **TQ39168 38311**

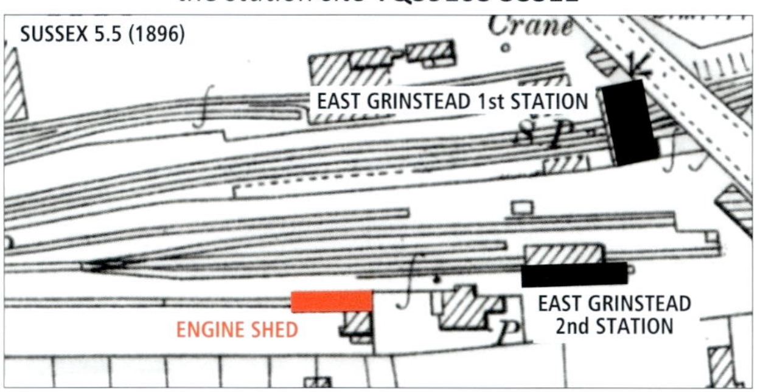

ERIDGE

Opened 3 August 1868 by the Brighton, Uckfield & Tunbridge Wells Railway. *(Platforms 1 & 2). Shared with* **ERIDGE** *[Spa Valley Railway] (Platform 3)*
TQ54240 34519

ETCHINGHAM

Opened 1 September 1851 by the SER.
TQ71459 26301

FOREST ROW

Opened 1 October 1866 by the East Grinstead, Groombridge & Tunbridge Wells Railway and closed 2 January 1967 by BR.

Line lifted - Demolished - Some platforms extant – Station site in commercial use **TQ42835 35287**

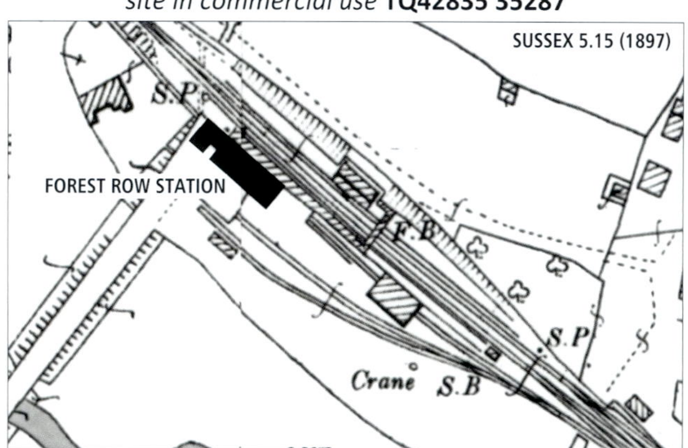

FRANT

Opened 1 September 1851 by the SER.
TQ60727 36369

GLYNDE

Opened 27 June 1846 by the London & Brighton Railway.
TQ45796 08667

HAMPDEN PARK

Opened 2 January 1888 by the LB&SCR as *Willingdon*, renamed as *Hampden Park for Willingdon* 1 July 1903, as *Hampden Park* by BR, as *Hampden Park Sussex* 12 May 1980 and reverted to *Hampden Park* in c1993.
TQ60760 02061

GROOMBRIDGE

Opened 1 October 1866 by the Brighton, Uxbridge & Tunbridge Wells Railway and closed 8 July 1985 by BR.
Line Operated by Spa Valley Railway - Station building in private use – Extended platforms incorporated in Spa Valley Railway station **TQ53306 37114**

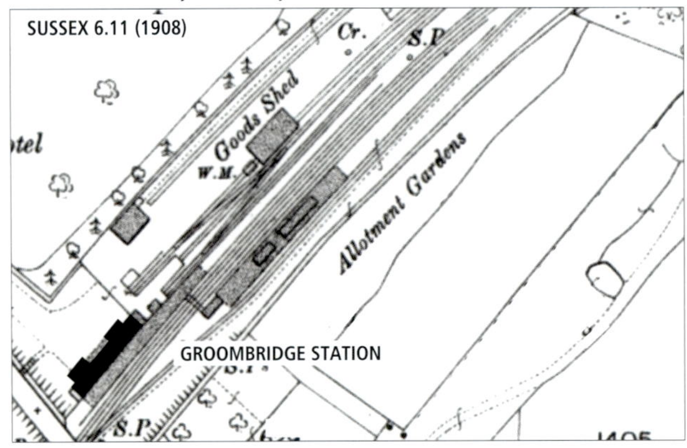

HARTFIELD

Opened 1 October 1866 by the East Grinstead, Groombridge & Tunbridge Railway and closed 2 January 1967 by BR. *Line lifted - Station building and platform in private use as "Hartfield Playschool"*
TQ47970 36210

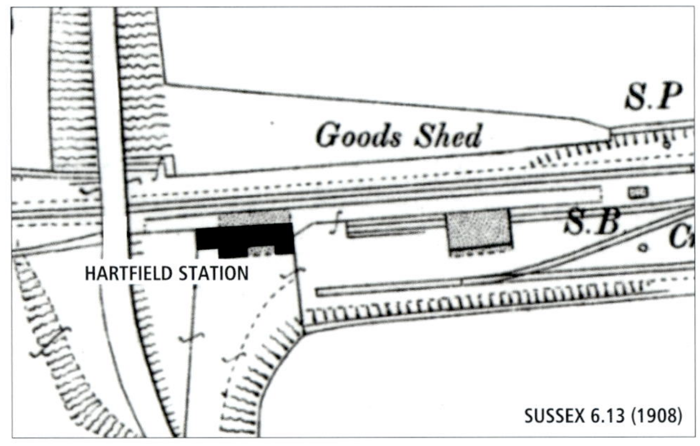

HAILSHAM

Opened 15 May 1849 by the LB&SCR and closed 9 September 1968 by BR.
Line lifted – Demolished – Station site occupied by housing in Lindfield Drive **TQ58952 09213**

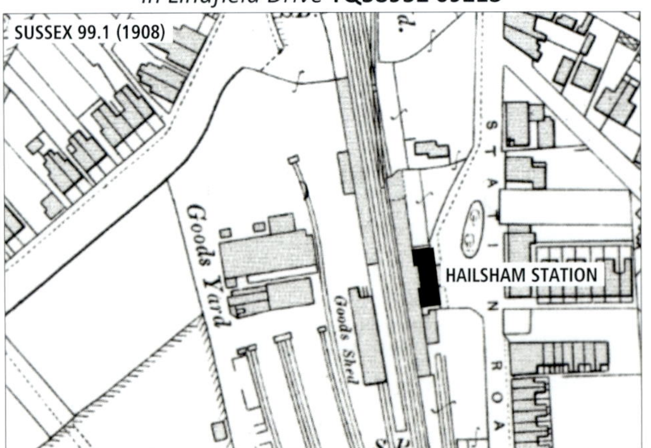

HASTINGS

Opened 13 February 1851 by the SER/LB&SCR.
TQ81464 09703

HEATHFIELD

Opened 5 April 1880 by the Tunbridge Wells & Eastbourne Railway and closed 14 June 1965 by BR.

Line lifted – Street-level station building in private use as a shop and café - The Cuckoo Trail passes through the station site **TQ58090 21306**

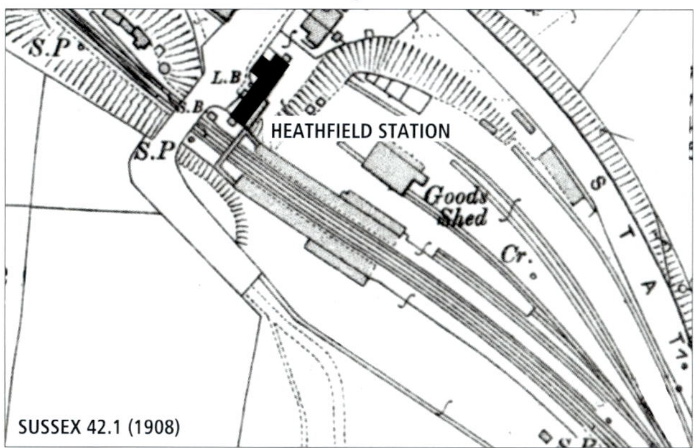

HELLINGLY

Opened 5 April 1880 by the Tunbridge Wells & Eastbourne Railway and closed 14 June 1965 by BR.

Line lifted - Station building and platform in private use - The Cuckoo Trail passes through the station site
TQ58470 12023

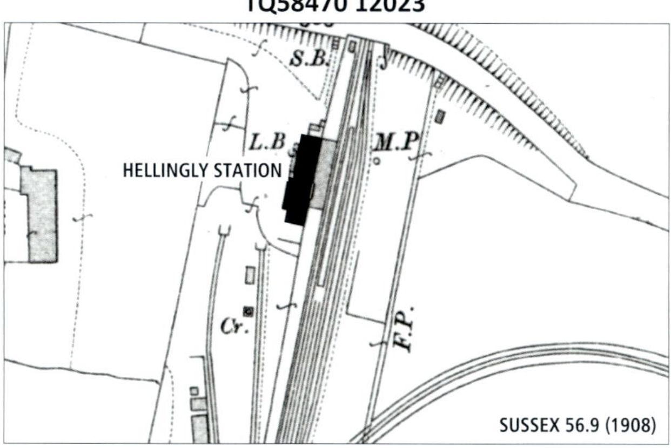

HIGH ROCKS HALT

Opened 1 June 1907 by the LB&SCR, closed 16 October 1939 by the SR, reopened 15 June 1942 and finally closed 5 May 1952 by BR.

Line Operated by the Spa Valley Railway – Demolished
TQ55933 38396

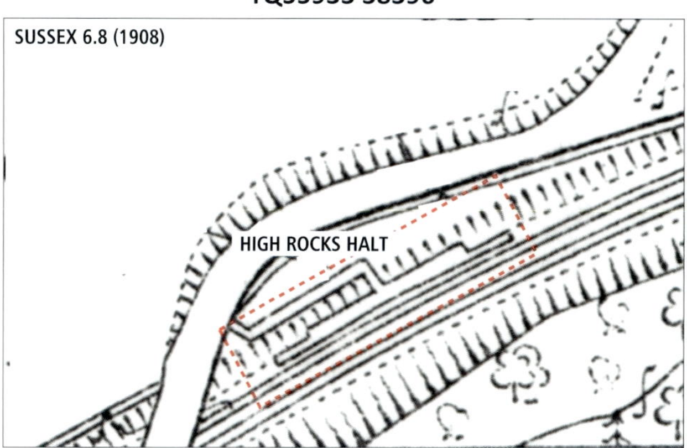

HORSTED KEYNES

Opened 1 August 1882 by the Lewes & East Grinstead Railway and closed for BR services 28 October 1963.
TQ37148 29254

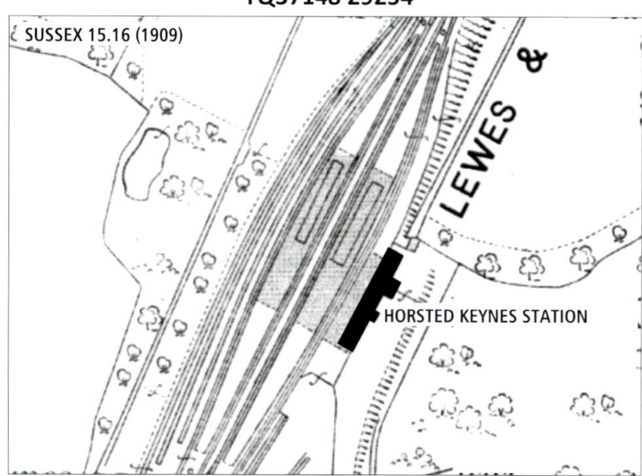

ISFIELD

Opened 18 October 1858 by the Lewes & Uckfield Railway closed 24 February 1969 by BR and sold for preservation 16 June 1983. **TQ45211 17116**

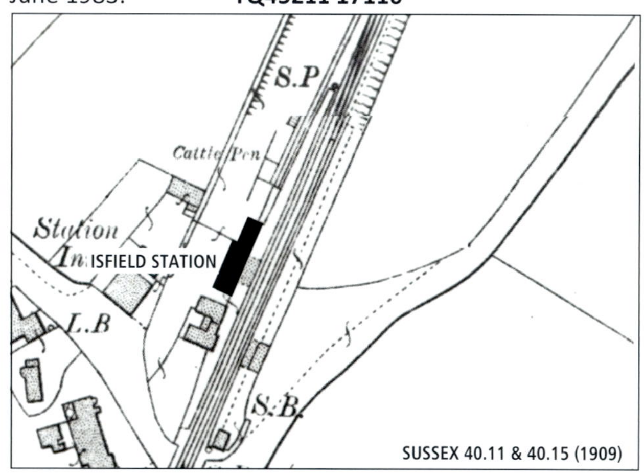

JUNCTION ROAD HALT

Opened in January 1901 by the Rother Valley Light Railway closed in May 1901, reopened in June 1903 and closed 4 January 1954 by BR.

Line lifted – Demolished – Station site being restored
TQ77118 24289

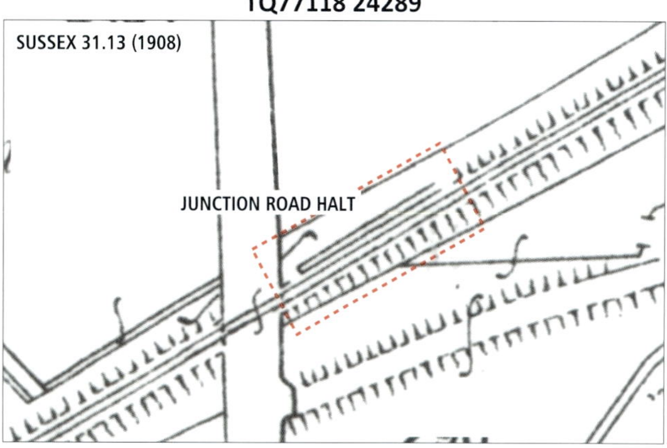

KINGSCOTE

Opened 1 August 1882 by the Lewes & East Grinstead Railway, closed 30 May 1955 by BR, reopened 7 August 1956, closed 17 March 1958 and finally reopened 23 April 1994 by the Bluebell Railway.
TQ36731 35568

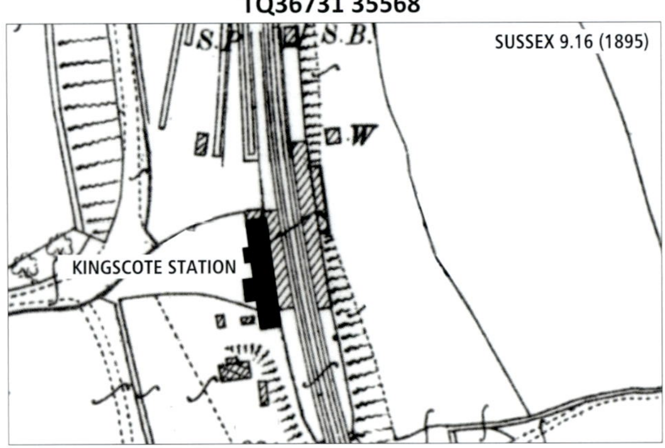

LEWES (1st)

Opened 1 November 1857 by the LB&SCR and closed 4 March 1889.
Line Operational **TQ41653 09832**

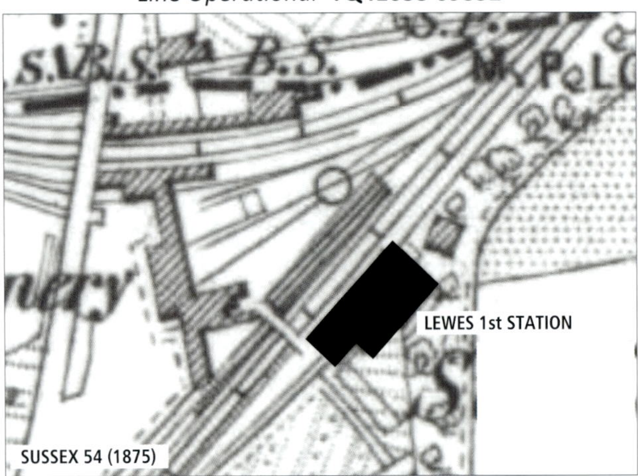

LEWES

Opened 4 March 1899 by the LB&SCR.
TQ41653 09832

LEWES FRIARS WALK

Opened 8 June 1846 by the London & Brighton Railway and closed 1 November 1857 by the LB&SCR.
Line lifted – Demolished – Station site occupied by dwellings in Court Road **TQ41857 10153**

LEWES HAM

Opened 8 June 1846 by the London & Brighton Railway and closed 1 November 1857 by the LB&SCR.
Line lifted – Demolished – Station site occupied by dwellings in Pinwell Road **TQ41738 09927**

LEWES PINWELL

Opened 1 October 1847 by the LB&SCR and closed 1 November 1857.
Line lifted – Demolished – Station site occupied by dwellings in Greyfriars Court **TQ41927 10075**

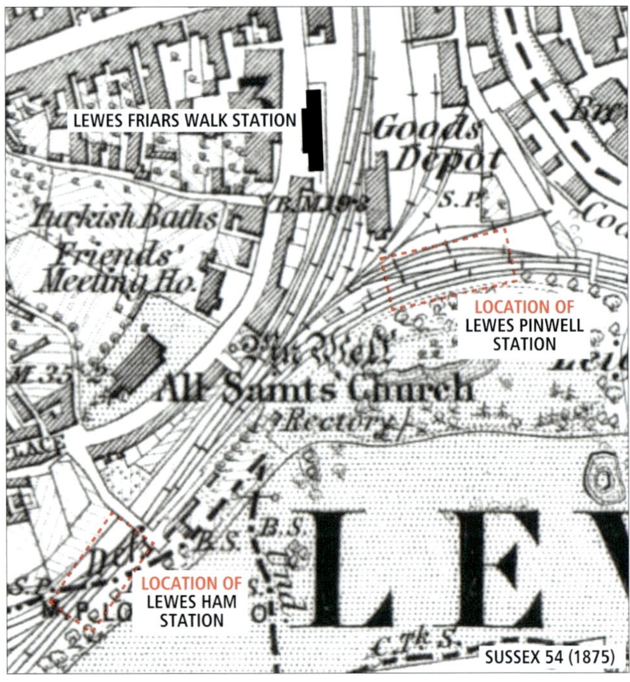

MAYFIELD

Opened 1 September 1880 by the Tunbridge Wells & Eastbourne Railway and closed 14 June 1965.
Line lifted - Station building in private use - The A267, Mayfield By-pass, passes through the station site at a lower level **TQ57846 26750**

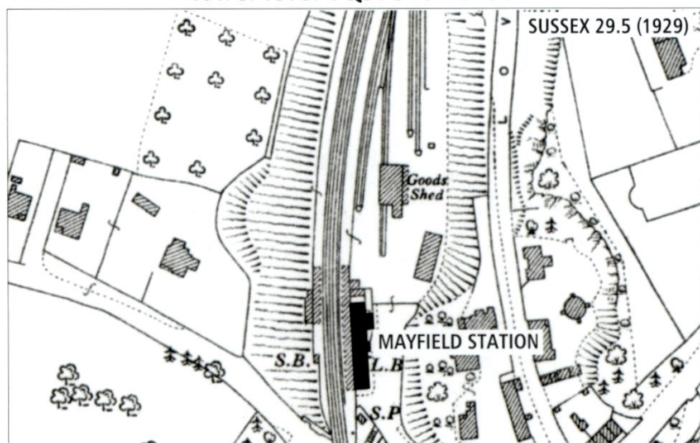

MOUNTFIELD HALT

Opened 1 August 1923 by the SR as *Mountfield Halt*, renamed as *Mountfield* 5 May 1969 by BR and closed 6 October 1969.

Line Operational – Demolished **TQ74556 19728**

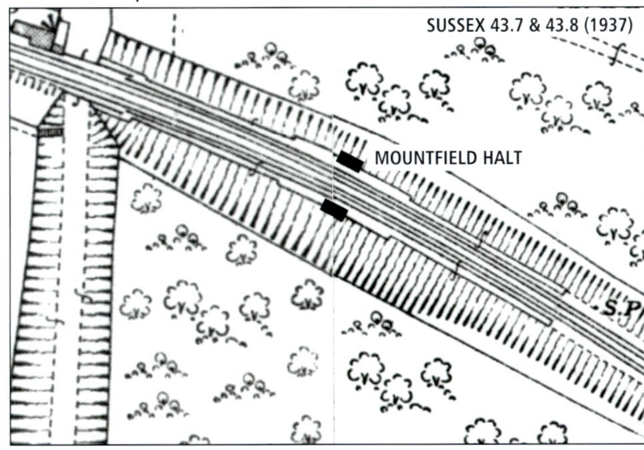

NEWHAVEN TOWN

Opened 8 December 1847 by the LB&SCR as *Newhaven* and renamed as *Newhaven Town* in 1864.

TQ44934 01490

NEWHAVEN HARBOUR

Opened 17 May 1846 by the LB&SCR, closed in August 1914 and reopened 14 August 1919.

TQ44947 00931

NEWHAVEN WHARF FOR PARIS

Opened 8 December 1847 by the LB&SCR and closed 17 May 1886.

Line lifted – Demolished – Station site in commercial use

TQ44970 00821

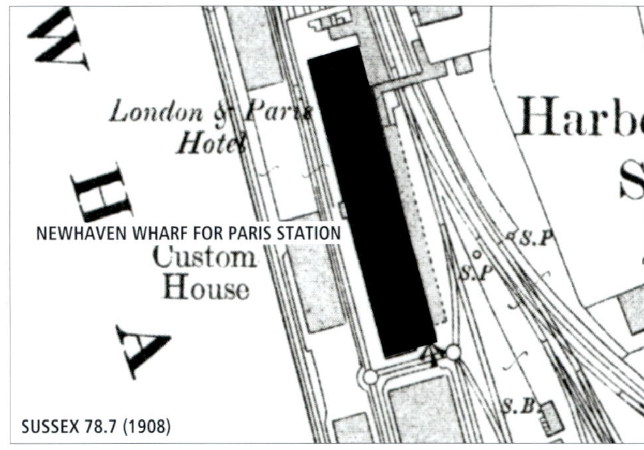

NEWHAVEN MARINE

Opened 17 May 1886 by the LB&SCR as *Newhaven East Quay*, subsequently renamed as *Newhaven Harbour Boat Station*, as *Newhaven Marine* 14 May 1984 by BR, closed and reopened intermittently from 11 November 1995 until final closure 22 October 2020 by Network Rail.

Line Out of Use – Demolished – No access

TQ45054 00718

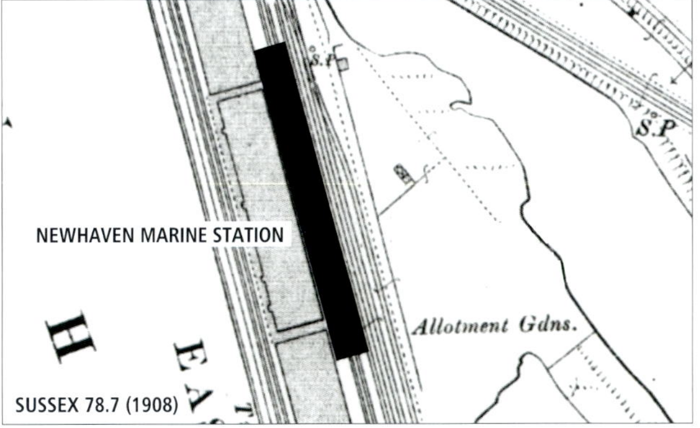

NEWICK & CHAILEY

Opened 1 August 1882 by the Lewes & East Grinstead Railway, closed 30 May 1955 by BR, reopened 7 August 1956 and finally closed 17 March 1958.

Line lifted – Demolished – Station site unused

TQ40135 20914

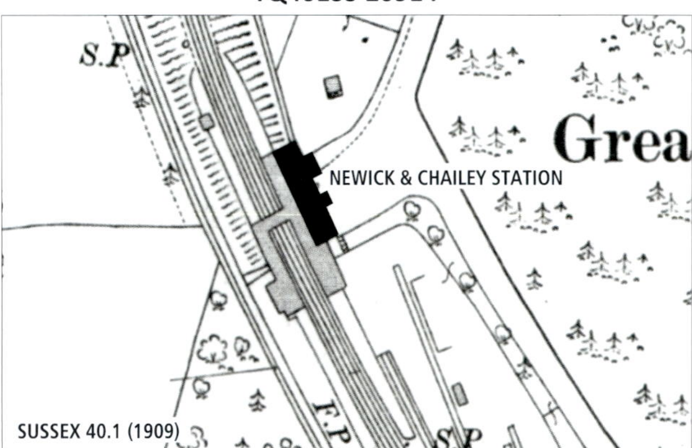

NORMANS BAY

Opened 11 September 1905 by the LB&SCR as *Normans Bay Halt* and renamed as *Normans Bay* 5 May 1969 by BR.
TQ68378 05663

PEVENSEY & WESTHAM

Opened 27 June 1846 by the LB&SCR as *West Ham & Pevensey* and renamed as *Pevensey & Westham* 1 January 1890.   **TQ63880 04379**

NORTHIAM

Opened 2 April 1900 by the Rother Valley Light Railway, closed 4 January 1954 by BR and reopened 19 May 1990 by the Kent & East Sussex Railway Preservation Society.
TQ83510 26601

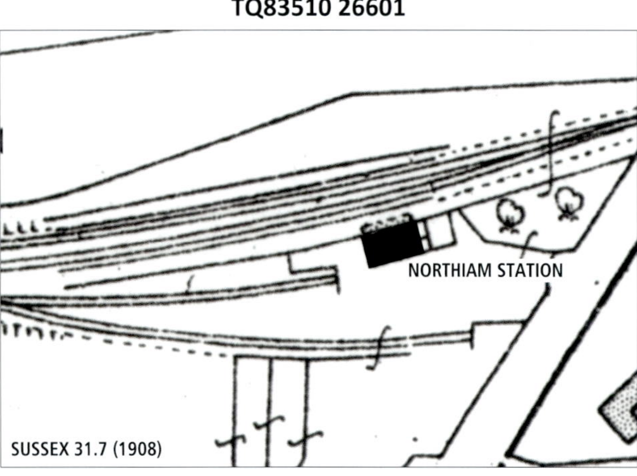

PEVENSEY BAY

Opened 11 September 1905 by the LB&SCR as *Pevensey Bay Halt* and renamed as *Pevensey Bay* 5 May 1969 by BR.
TQ65133 04627

ORE

Opened 1 January 1888 by the SER.
TQ82476 10691

POLEGATE

Opened 3 October 1881 by the LB&SCR and closed 25 May 1986 by BR.
Line Operational – Demolished – No access
TQ58646 04800

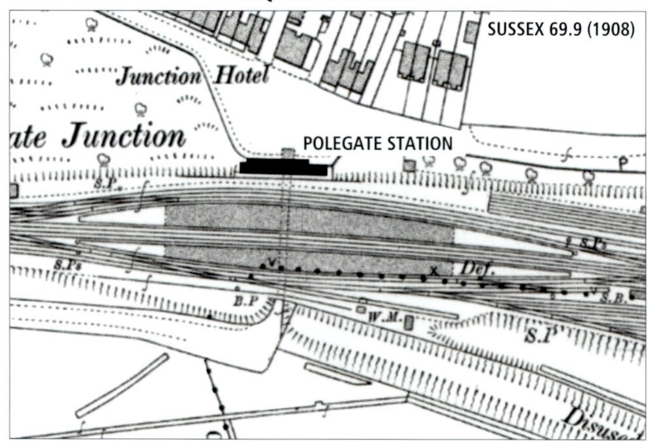

POLEGATE

Opened 27 June 1846 by the London & Brighton Railway closed 3 October 1881 by the LB&SCR and reopened 25 May 1986 by BR.   **TQ58310 04804**

ROBERTSBRIDGE

Opened 1 September 1851 by the SER.
TQ73375 23582

ROBERTSBRIDGE JUNCTION

Opened 2 April 1900 by the Rother Valley Light Railway and closed 4 January 1954 by BR.
TQ73375 23582

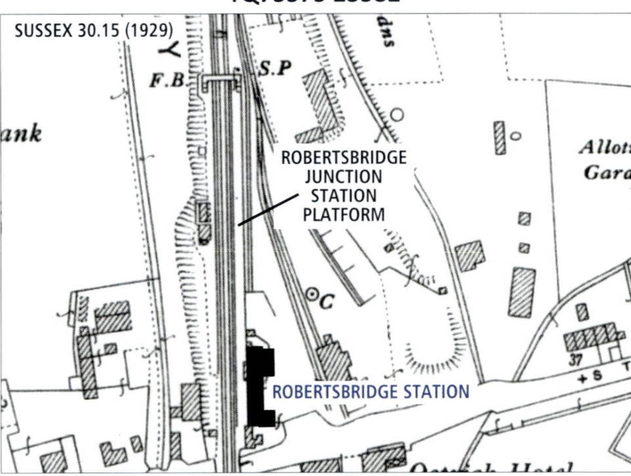

ROTHERFIELD & MARK CROSS

Opened 1 September 1880 by the Tunbridge Wells & Eastbourne Railway as *Rotherfield*, renamed as *Rotherfield & Mark Cross* 1 November 1901 by the SE&CR and closed 14 June 1965 by BR.
Line lifted - Station building and platforms in private use
TQ56569 30294

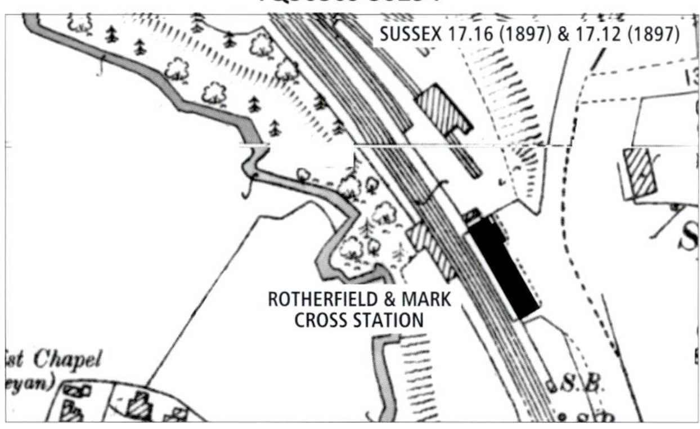

RYE

Opened 13 February 1851 by the SER.
TQ91917 20574

ST LEONARDS WARRIOR SQUARE

Opened 13 February 1851 by the SER as *St Leonards*, renamed as *St Leonards Warrior Square* 5 December 1870, closed 1 January 1917 by the SE&CR and reopened 1 January 1919.   **TQ80333 09380**

ST LEONARDS WEST MARINA
(1st)

Opened 7 November 1846 by the London & Brighton Railway as *Hastings & St Leonards*, renamed as *St Leonards* 13 February 1851 by the LB&SCR, as *St Leonards West Marina* 5 December 1870 and closed 1 June 1889.

Line Operational – Demolished – No access
TQ78535 08849

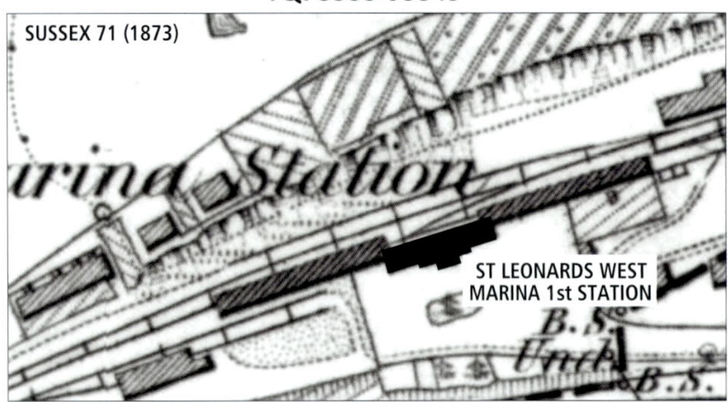

ST LEONARDS WEST MARINA

Opened 1 June 1889 by the LB&SCR and closed 10 July 1967 by BR.

Line Operational – Demolished - Eastbound platform extant - No access **TQ78656 08890**

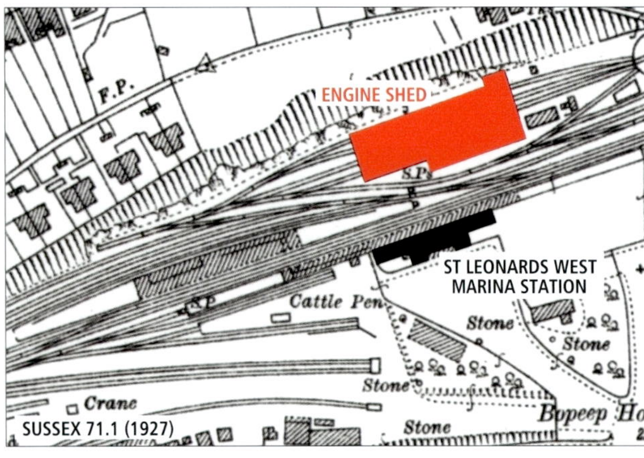

SALEHURST HALT

Opened 23 September 1929 by the Kent & East Sussex Railway as *Salehurst*, renamed as *Salehurst Platform* in 1929, as *Salehurst* in c1932, as *Salehurst Halt* in 1939 and closed 4 January 1954 by BR.

Line lifted – Demolished – Station site unused
TQ74947 24077

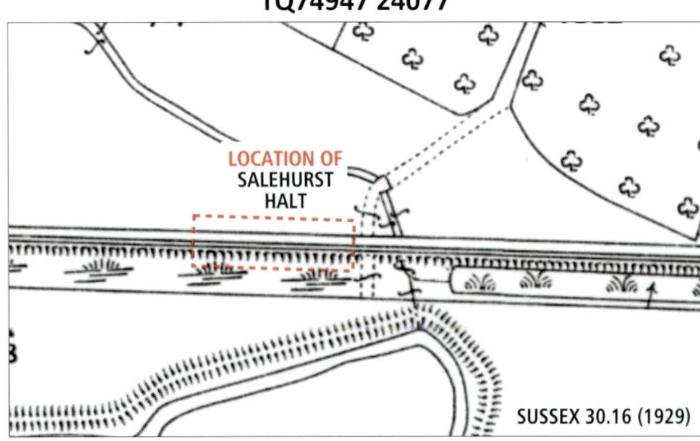

SEAFORD

Opened 1 June 1864 by the LB&SCR.
TV48156 99139

SHEFFIELD PARK

Opened 1 August 1882 by the Lewes & East Grinstead Railway as *Fletching & Sheffield Park*, renamed as *Sheffield Park* 1 January 1883 by the LB&SCR, closed 30 May 1955 by BR, reopened 7 August 1956, closed 17 March 1958 and reopened 31 July 1960 by the Bluebell Railway.
TQ40365 23681

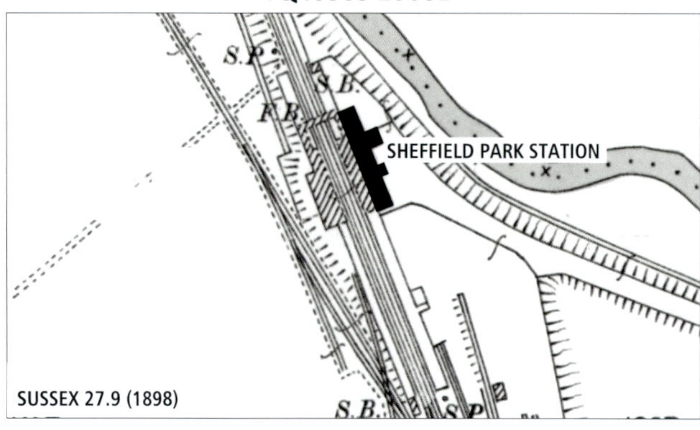

SIDLEY

Opened 1 June 1902 by the Crowhurst, Sidley & Bexhill Railway, closed 1 January 1917 by the SE&CR, reopened 14 June 1920 and finally closed 15 June 1964 by BR.

Line lifted – Demolished - The A2690, Combe Valley Way, passes through the station site **TQ74274 09008**

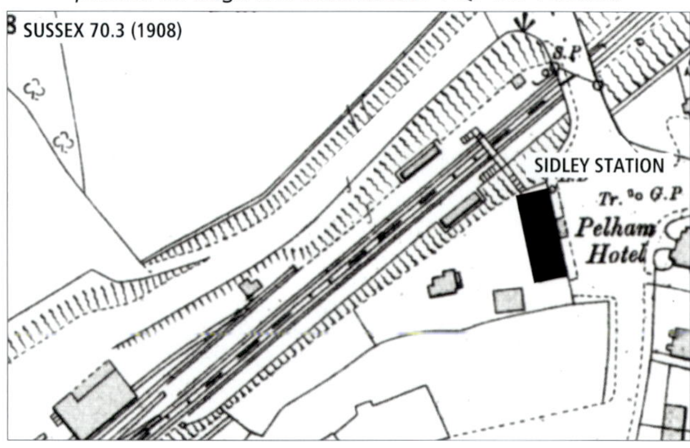

SNAILHAM HALT

Opened 1 July 1907 by the SE&CR and closed 2 February 1959 by BR.

Line Operational – Demolished - No access

TQ85869 17479

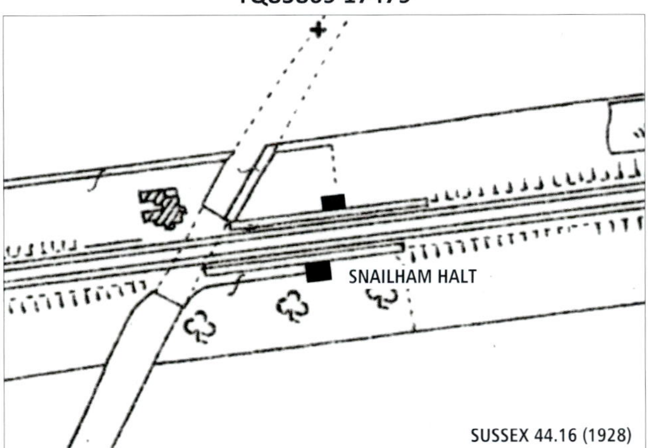

STONEGATE

Opened 1 September 1851 by the SER as *Witherenden*, renamed as *Ticehurst Road* in December 1851 and as *Stonegate* 16 June 1947 by the SR.

TQ65878 27170

SOUTHEASE

Opened 1 September 1906 by the LB&SCR as *Southease & Rodmell Halt*, renamed as *Southease & Rodmell* 5 May 1969 and as *Southease* 12 May 1980.

TQ43100 05492

THREE OAKS

Opened 1 July 1907 by the SE&CR as *Three Oaks Bridge Halt*, subsequently renamed as *Three Oaks Halt*, as *Three Oaks & Guestling Halt* in 1908 and as *Three Oaks* 5 May 1969 by BR.

TQ83836 14541

STONE CROSS HALT

Opened 11 September 1905 by the LB&SCR and closed 7 July 1935 by the SR.

Line Operational – Demolished – No access

TQ61857 04007

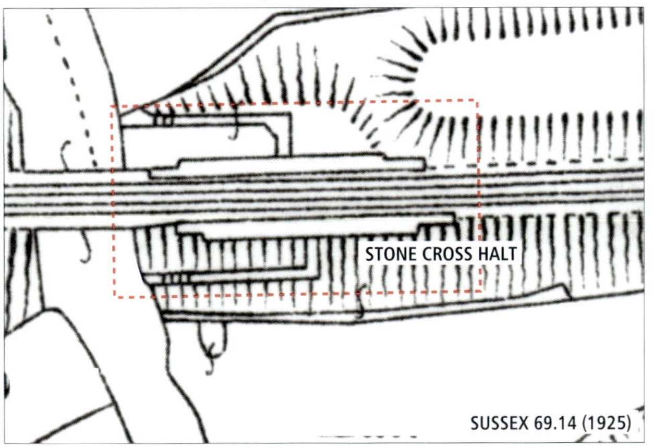

UCKFIELD

Opened 18 October 1858 by the Lewes & Uckfield Railway and closed 13 May 1991 by BR.

Line lifted – Demolished – Station site unused

TQ47190 20876

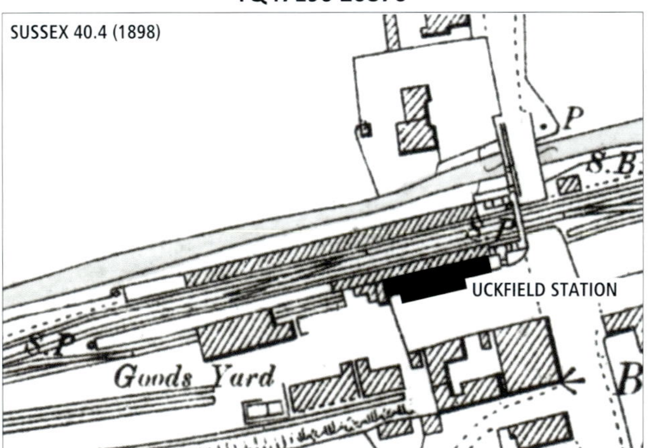

UCKFIELD

Opened 13 May 1991 by BR.
TQ47315 20910

WADHURST

Opened 1 September 1851 by the SER.
TQ62168 32961

WALDRON & HORAM

Opened 5 April 1880 by the Tunbridge Wells & Eastbourne Railway as *Horeham Road for Waldron*, renamed as *Horeham Road & Waldron* 1 June 1890 by the LB&SCR, as *Waldron & Horeham Road* 1 April 1900, as *Waldron & Horam* 1 January 1935 by the SR, as *Horam* 21 September 1953 by BR and closed 14 June 1965.
Line lifted – Demolished - The Cuckoo Trail passes through the station site **TQ57871 17466**

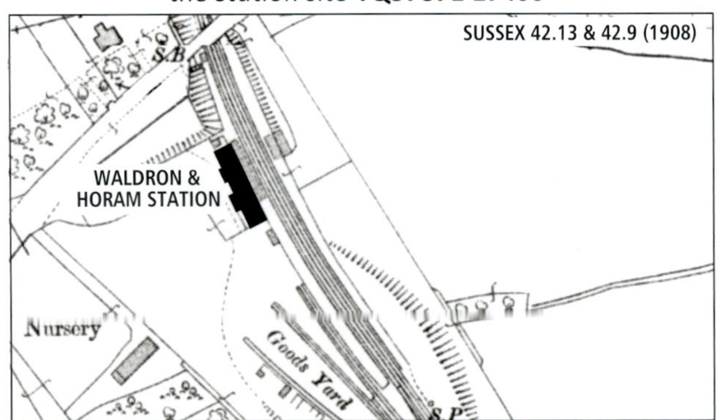

WEST HOATHLY

Opened 1 August 1882 by the Lewes & East Grinstead Railway, closed 30 May 1955 by BR, reopened 7 August 1956 and finally closed 17 March 1958.
Line Operated by the Bluebell Railway – Demolished
TQ37137 32851

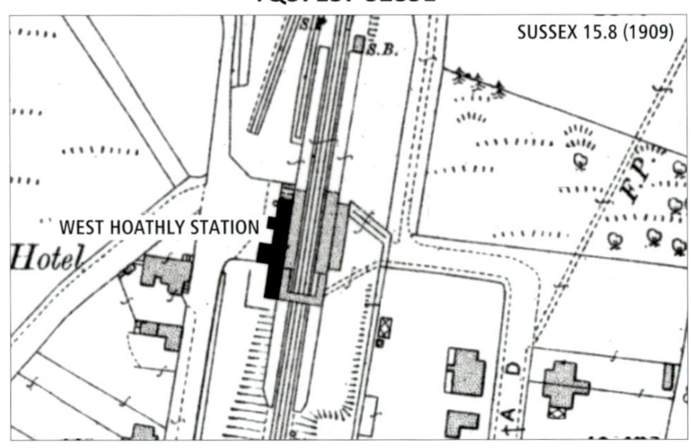

WEST ST LEONARDS

Opened 1 October 1887 by the SER.
TQ78883 09042

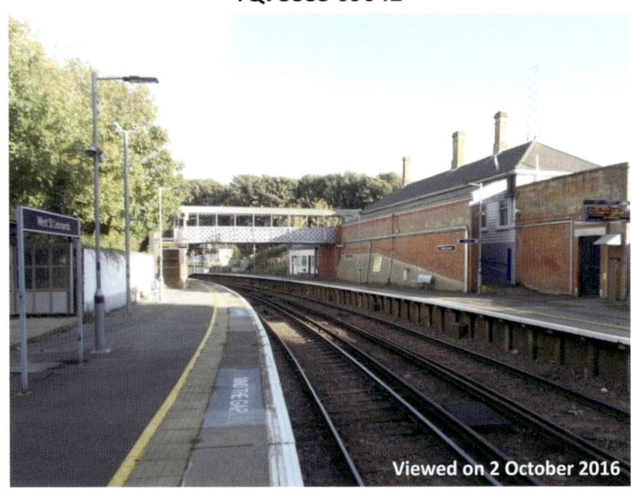

WINCHELSEA

Opened 13 February 1851 by the SER as *Winchelsea*, closed 1 September 1851, reopened 1 January 1852, renamed as *Winchelsea Halt* 12 September 1961 by BR and reverted to *Winchelsea* 5 May 1969.
TQ89985 18409

WITHYHAM

Opened 1 October 1866 by the East Grinstead, Groombridge & Tunbridge Wells Railway and closed 2 January 1967 by BR.

Line lifted - Station building and platform in private use - The Forest Way cycle/walkway passes through the station site **TQ49919 36439**

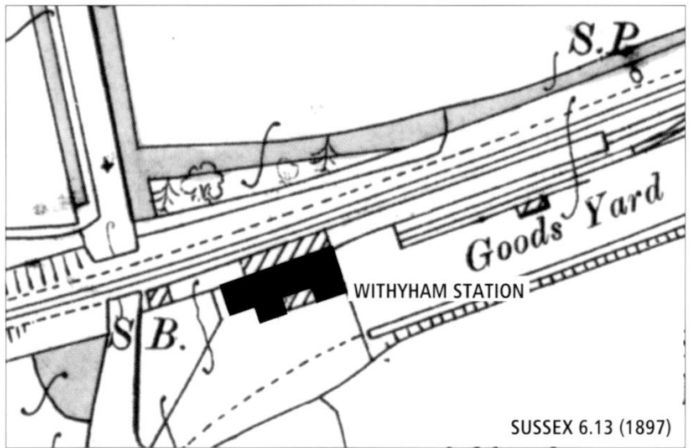

BIBLIOGRAPHY

Railway Atlas Then and Now by Paul Smith & Keith Turner Crécy Publishing Third Edition (2020). ISBN 978-0-86093-698-5

Railway Passenger Stations in Great Britain: A Chronology by Michael Quick. Railway & Canal Historical Society (2009). ISBN 978-0-901461-57-5

The Directory of Railway Stations by RVJ Butt. Patrick Stephens Ltd (1995). ISBN 1-85260-508-1

British Railway Stations 1825-1900: An Essential Gazetteer by Paul Smith & Sally Salmon. Unique Books (2023) ISBN 978-1-913555-15-3

British Railway Stations Since 1901: An Essential Gazetteer by Paul Smith & Sally Salmon. Unique Books (2022) ISBN 978-1-913555-11-5

WEBSITES ACCESSED

Disused Stations: http://disused-stations.org.uk/
National Library of Scotland: www.nls.uk

Maps sourced from the Cambridge University Map Library are reproduced by permission of the Syndics of Cambridge University.

The single platform and main station building at Barcombe viewed looking towards the north. *J. Joyce/Online Transport Archive*

Viewed looking towards the north on 8 May 1977, some seven years after track lifting on the line, Barcombe Mills remains largely intact. Some 50 years on, the main station building remains although the Down wooden waiting room was demolished in 2003. *John Hayward/Online Transport Archive*

Class L 4-4-0 No 31774 pictured at Battle with the 3.28pm service from Tonbridge to Hastings on 14 September 1953.
Donald Kelk/Online Transport Archive

On 15 March 1958 Class H 0-4-4T No 31269 awaits departure from Bexhill West for a service to Crowhurst. *Peter N. Williams/Online Transport Archive*
Bodiam station pictured from the east on 18 April 1953. *Neil Davenport/Online Transport Archive*

Class 2BIL No 2091 approaches Cooden Beach from the west with a Down service towards Hastings in 1958. *Fred Ivey/Online Transport Archive*

Class H 0-4-4T No 31295 about to depart from the Up platform at Crowhurst in 1958. *Fred Ivey/Online Transport Archive*

The proximity of the High Level and Low Level platforms at East Grinstead could not be more starkly demonstrated than in this view of 'H' class 0-4-4T 31530 departing with a service to Three Bridges on 15 March 1958. *Gerald Druce/Online Transport Archive*

BR Standard 2-6-4T No 80145 is pictured running round its train at Eastbourne station on 8 June 1965. *Rev A. M. Logan/Online Transport Archive*

On 22 May 1985 Class 205 No 1120 awaits departure from platform 3 at Eridge station. *Geoffrey Tribe/Online Transport Archive*

On 19 August 1956 2-6-4T No 42105 stands at Groombridge station with a westbound service towards Victoria from Tunbridge Wells. *Peter N. Williams/Online Transport Archive*

'West Country' No 34019 *Bideford* pictured with a two-coach train from Eastbourne at Hailsham in May 1960. *Derek Cross*

On 30 May 1958 'Schools' class No 30924 *Haileybury* awaits departure from Hastings with the 7.10pm service to Charing Cross.
Bernard Harrison/Bob Bridger Collection/Online Transport Archive

Horsted Keynes station on 16 March 1958. *Charles Firminger/Bob Bridger Collection/Online Transport Archive*

An undated view, taken from the north, of the LBSCR station at Isfield; this is now the terminus of the preserved Lavender Line.
John Meredith Collection/Online Transport Archive

Pictured in May 1962 looking towards the north, post closure, the tracks at Kingscote awaiting lifting. The lines were lifted the following year but relayed as part of the Bluebell Railway's northern extension. *Roy Hobbs/Online Transport Archive*

In 1958 Class D1 4-4-0 31470 awaits departure with a westbound service at Lewes. *Fred Ivey/Online Transport Archive*

On 17 July 1965 Class HA (later Class 71) No E5002 approaches Newhaven Harbour from the east light engine. *John Meredith/Online Transport Archive*

Newick & Chailey station viewed from the south on 16 March 1958. Until the 1930s, when they were removed, there were buildings on the Up platform as well as a footbridge linking the two platforms. *Charles Firminger/Bob Bridger Collection/Online Transport Archive*

On 10 June 1966 Class 3H (later Class 205) DEMU No 1116 is pictured departing Polegate with a service towards Eastbourne. *John Meredith/Online Transport Archive*

During 1958 Class U 2-6-0 31900 is seen at Robertsbridge with a Down service. *Fred Ivey/Online Transport Archive*

On 11 June 1965, shortly before closure, a Standard 2-6-4T is pictured awaiting departure from Rotherfield & Mark Cross with a Down service. *Rev A. M. Logan/Online Transport Archive*

The exterior of the main station building at Rye in 1989. *Geoffrey Tribe/Online Transport Archive*

Connex Class 4CIG No 1740 is pictured with a westbound service at St Leonards Warrior Square in May 2000. *John Law/Online Transport Archive*

The view along the platform at Seaford station towards the west in 1989; the signal box at the platform end was eventually demolished in 2002. *Geoffrey Tribe/Online Transport Archive*

The approach to Sheffield Park station on 16 March 1958. *Charles Firminger/Bob Bridger Collection/Online Transport Archive*

Push-pull set No 661 leads with a Down service towards Bexhill West at Sidley in 1958. *Fred Ivey/Online Transport Archive*

West Hoathley station viewed from the south in May 1962; at this date the line had closed but the rusting track awaited lifting.
Roy Hobbs/Online Transport Archive

A Day in the Life

Photographs by Neil Davenport/Online Transport Archive

BR inherited all 40 of the Drummond-designed Class L11 4-4-0s but when No 158 was recorded on the day it had recently been taken out of service and placed in store. Although 1949 was to witness the first withdrawals of the class, No 158 — which was never to receive its BR number — was not one of those to suffer that fate, being reinstated and reallocated to Guildford in June 1949. It was to remain based there for some 18 months prior to withdrawal in December 1950; it was scrapped later the same month. The last of the class were withdrawn during 1952.

On 31 December 1948 — the last day of the first year of the nationalised railway — Neil Davenport visited Feltham shed and recorded the considerable variety of locomotives that were awaiting their next duties.

Pictured stored was WD 2-10-0 No 73776; this was one of the two of the class — the other being No 73774 — that were restored to traffic during the spring and summer of 1948 for use in the Locomotive Exchanges as BR undertook comparative trials of the locomotives that it inherited. No 73776 was tested between Toton and Brent during June 1948 whilst No 73774 was used more widely two months later, including operation between Eastleigh and Bristol. Both were transferred to BR, becoming Nos 90750 (ex-73774) and 90752 (ex-73776) and entered service at Motherwell in February 1949. No 90752 was finally withdrawn in December 1961.

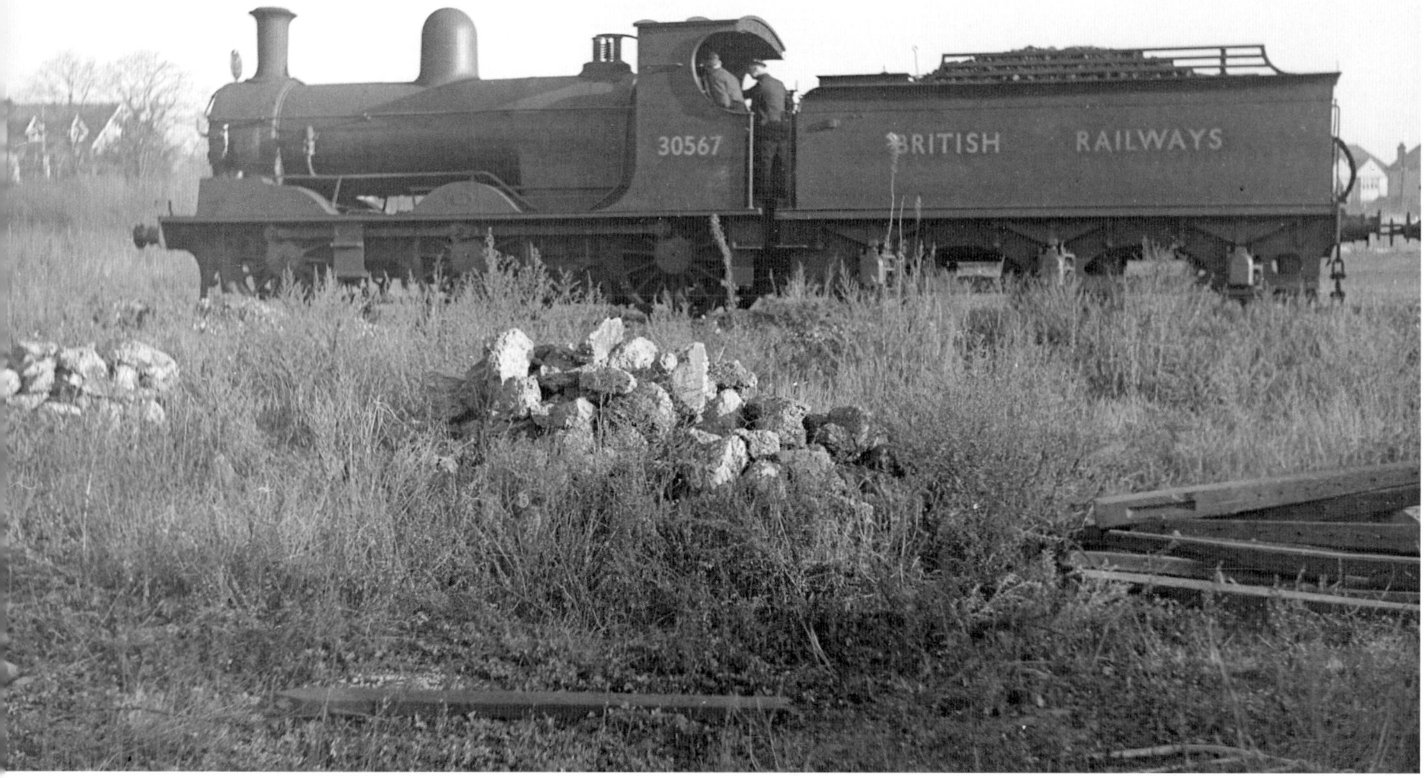
30567
BRITISH RAILWAYS

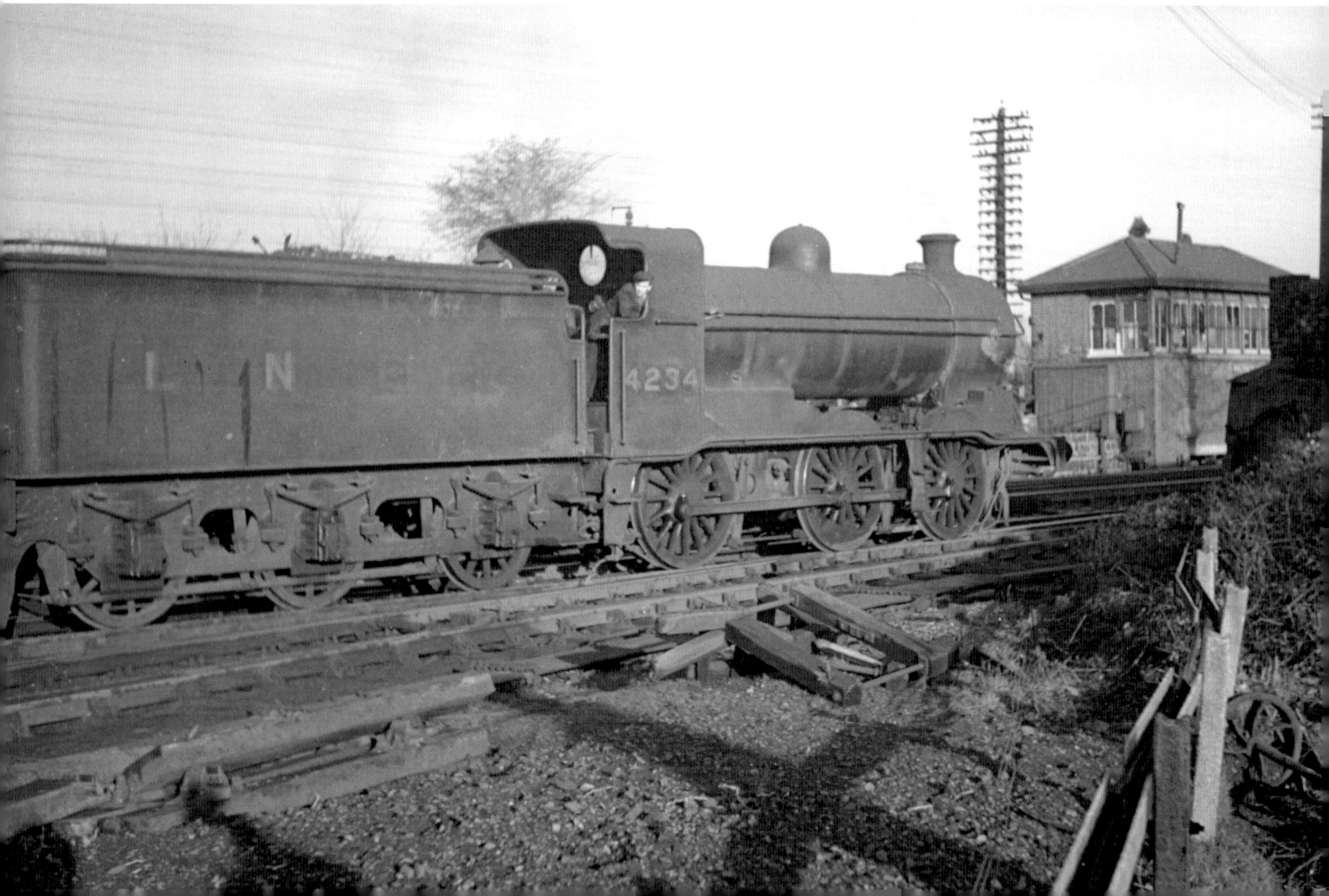
4234

Also still bearing its Southern number and identity was Class S15 No 458. Although based at Feltham on nationalisation, the 4-6-0 had migrated to Nine Elms during the spring of the year; it was allocated to that shed until early 1950 when it returned to Feltham where it was to remain until withdrawal in mid-June 1963.

Opposite top: **Adams-designed 'Jumbo' 0-6-0 No 30567 was an early recipient of its BR number and identity, being renumbered in March 1948. It was to be based at Feltham throughout its BR career until withdrawal in early December 1959 (the last of the class to be taken out of service), having been reallocated to the shed in December 1935. Of the 70-strong Class 0395 that was introduced in 1881, only 18 passed into BR ownership — 50 having been transferred to the government in 1916 for military use in the Middle East and two being withdrawn by the Southern Railway — but this long-lived class was operational for almost 80 years.**

Bottom: **It was not only ex-Southern locomotives that were present on the day; in addition to a number of ex-War Department locomotives, ex-LNER Class J6 0-6-0 No 4234 — still unrenumbered — was also at work with an inter-regional freight. Based at Hornsey when recorded here, the locomotive dated originally to August 1914. It was reallocated to the ex-Great Central Thrumpton shed at Grantham in March 1951 from where it was withdrawn in mid-December 1959.**

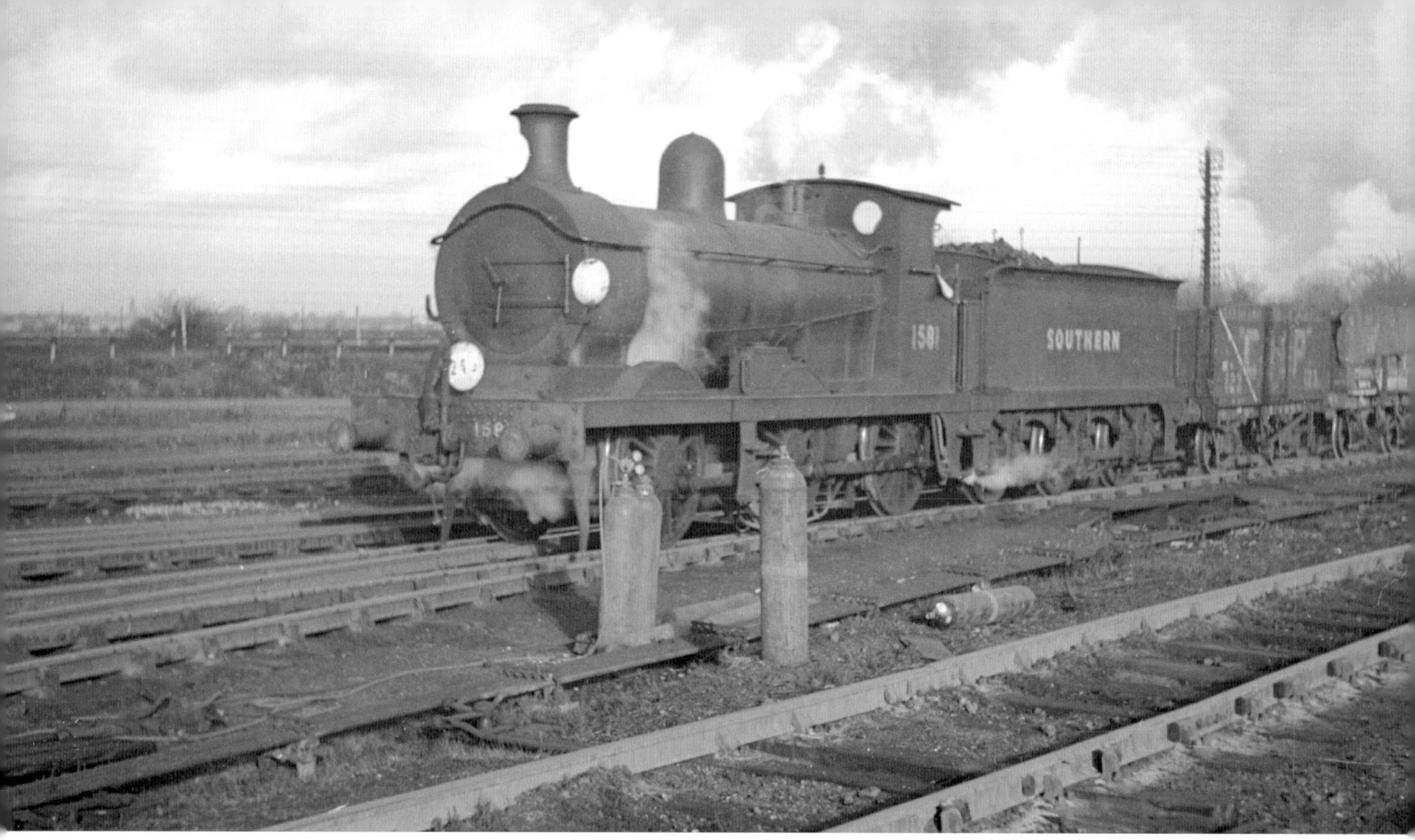
1581
SOUTHERN

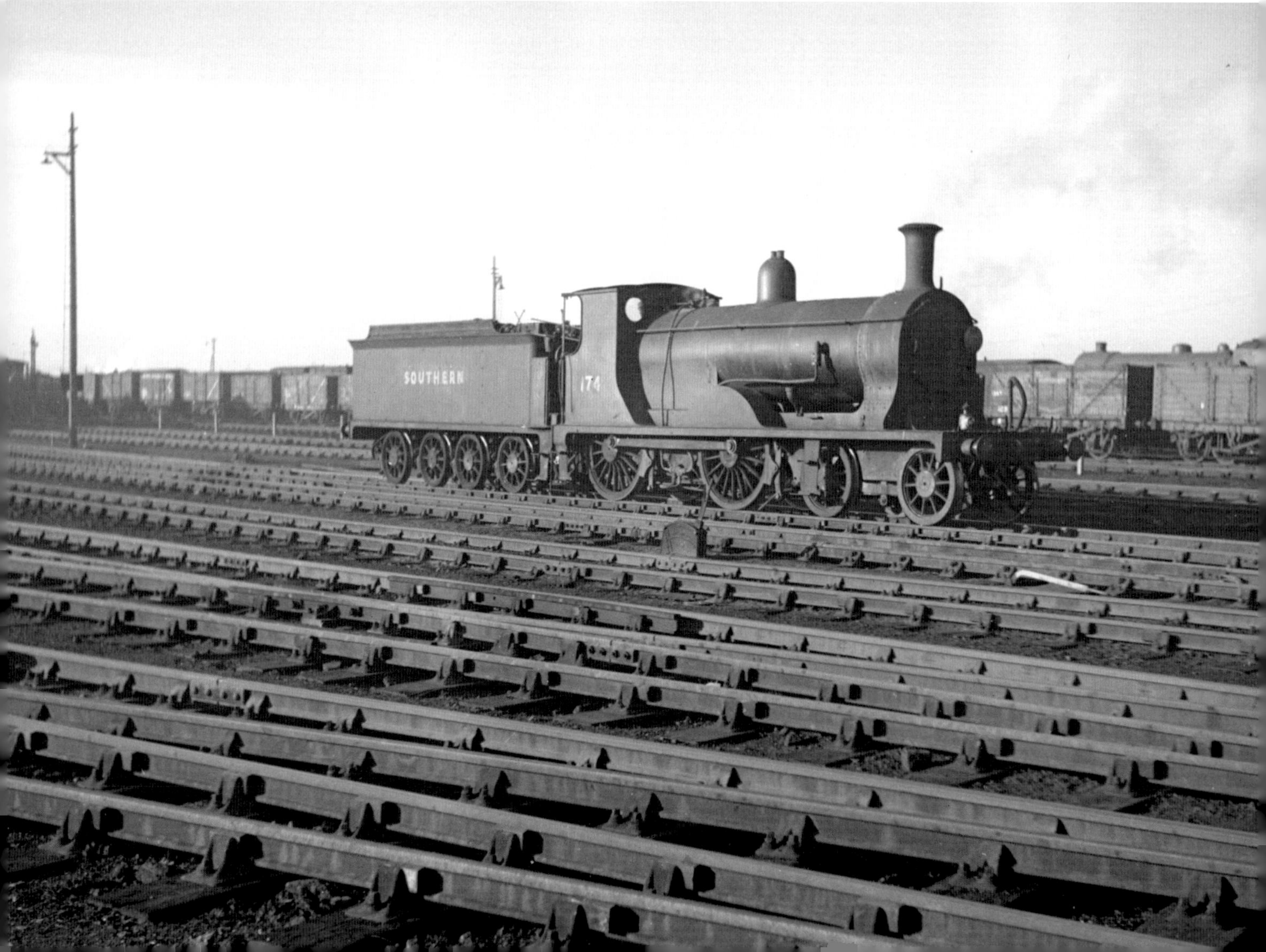
SOUTHERN
174

Bearing 'British Railways' on the tender but showing its original Southern number with an 'S' prefix was Class S15 No S838. Delivered new to Hither Green from Eastleigh Works in May 1936, the 4-6-0 was to spend the bulk of its career allocated to Feltham following its transfer there in October 1939. In early 1965 the 4-6-0 was briefly based at Eastleigh but it quickly returned to Feltham from where it was withdrawn in mid-September 1965.

Opposite top: **Class C No 1581 was recorded with a freight; this Wainwright-designed locomotive was new to the SECR in May 1903 having been completed at Ashford Works. When pictured here the 0-6-0 was allocated to Hither Green; it was destined to remain there until July 1951 — having gained its BR number exactly two years earlier — when it was transferred to Stewarts Lane from where it was withdrawn in early March 1960.**

Bottom: **Another Class L11 on shed on 31 December was No 174, again still retaining its Southern number and identity. Based at Feltham throughout its BR career, the 4-4-0 was renumbered in January 1951 but was not to bear its BR number for long as it was withdrawn in September the same year.**

Another 'H15' to be recorded on the day, but by now renumbered, was No 30489, which had acquired its BR identity in May. Apart from a brief period in store at Eastleigh in late 1950, the 4-6-0 was to spend its entire BR life allocated to Nine Elms shed, from where it was withdrawn at the end of January 1961.

The 'Q1' class was explored more fully in *Southern Way 69*, but the future No 33009 was allocated to Feltham when recorded here, retaining its Southern number and lettering. The locomotive was based at Guildford at the start of the BR era but was transferred to Feltham three months later. Except for a two-month period during the spring of 1953, it was based at Feltham until September 1964; it was then transferred to Guildford for nine months before spending the last three months of its operational career, prior to withdrawal in late September 1965, at Nine Elms.

Another locomotive pictured in an intermediate stage — with BR lettering but with its Southern number prefixed by an 'S' — was Class G16 No S494. This was one of a class of four locomotives built at Eastleigh to a design of Robert Urie specifically for use at the newly completed marshalling yard at Feltham. All four were based at Feltham for their entire BR careers, being withdrawn between February 1959 and December 1962; No 30494 was one of two that lasted until the latter date. It was last recorded on the scrapline at Eastleigh in January 1963.

Another class of War Department locomotive seen on the day — but this time in use — was a 2-8-0, No 77108. Built by Vulcan Foundry (Works No 4924) as No 7108, the Riddles-designed locomotive was renumbered 77108 in early 1945. In early 1947, the 2-8-0 was noted at Brighton being prepared for operation for the LNER but was loaned initially to the Southern and based at Fratton; it was reallocated to Feltham in late 1947, where it was to remain until mid-1951. It was officially renumbered by BR as No 90570 in September 1950. Transferred to the London Midland Region, it was to be based at Aintree, Wigan Central, Newton Heath and Patricroft prior to being reallocated to Woodford Halse, on the Great Central, in early 1963. Except for a brief two-month sojourn at Kirkby-in-Ashfield in early 1964, it remained at Woodford Halse until withdrawal at the end of April that year. It was scrapped at Cashmore's, Great Bridge, six months later.

Index of locations

Corrigenda

A few comments and corrections to note for *Southern Way 71*; as always, many thanks to all who make contact. Stuart Hicks writes as follows:

Another enjoyable variety in *SW71* thank you, but in the topical SWR article I would suggest that:

    * On page 26 the main focus of use [for the Class 444 stock] has been (since 2007, when the Class 442 were withdrawn) on the Bournemouth and Weymouth route, although varying number of faster Portsmouth Harbour workings (both Portsmouth direct and some via Fareham) have and are formed of the stock,

    * Page 28, lower. Class 456 did not survive into the post-privatisation era; post covid formations were reduced and so as only 8 car trains were needed the 456s met an early end. (January 2022.)

David Hodge has noticed a few literals: on page 63 the locomotive is No 32626 and not No 32636 and on page 86 the Class 09 should be No 09018. In addition he's spotted that the opening of Amberley station on page 44 was incorrectly ascribed to the LSWR; it was, of course, the LBSCR.

Nick Stanbury has noticed an incorrect location in one image; he writes as follows: 'In issue 71 of *The Southern Way*, you correctly mention at page 6 the closure of the line between Bollo Lane Junction and Acton Lane Junction (formerly used by LMR goods/coal trains between Cricklewood and West Kensington or Kensington High Street). However, the associated lower photograph on page 12 is incorrectly captioned. It does not show a train 'on the curve from Bollo Lane Junction to Gunnersbury Junction', but on LMR territory between Acton Junction (with the corresponding signal box visible) and Kew East Junction (probably bound for Feltham Yard although the headcode does not appear correct). Moreover, the line to the right does not reach Bollo Lane Junction for some distance, after passing under the District/Piccadilly Lines overbridge The signal box at Acton Lane Junction was noteworthy in that, although at the boundary of former LSWR territory and still within the Southern Region, it had since the LSWR service ceased in 1915 only seen LMR and District Line trains.'

I'm also grateful to Stuart and to David for corrections to earlier issues.

David notes that on page 14 of issue 68, it is No 5941 and not No 5951 that is recorded at Lymington Pier. Although the wrong number was a literal, the narrative concerning the unit was correct; as shown, it was originally Class 2HAP No 6043 and was new in December 1958. It was one of two from that batch converted to Class 2SAP — the other being No 6044 (as No 5942 — and reverted to '2HAP' status in March 1980. From May 1982 it was combined with No 6046 as '4CAP' No 3302, which was finally withdrawn in April 1993 and scrapped in August the same year.

With regards to issue 70, David comments on the wartime damage to No 806 *Sir Galleron*; he writes: 'The incident was not quite as it is described here. The train was not hit by the V1. It was derailed when, travelling at speed, it reached a bridge which had been damaged only seconds before. For a full account of the incident see *Southern Way Special: 6 Wartime Southern Part 3* pages 77-83.' There were a few gremlins in the feature on Class 159s. On page 25, it was No 159102 that was involved in the accident at Fisherton Tunnel and not 1589012. On pages 30 and 31, the top caption should refer to the image on page 31; the middle caption covers the lower image on page 31, featuring No 159019 and not 158019, and the bottom caption should be disregarded. The caption for the image on page 30 records No 159106 approaching Clapham Junction with an Up service. There are a couple of literals: page 33 (top caption) it should read No 159101 and on page 34 (top) No 159102. Unfortunately, Petersfield is omitted from the feature on Southern stations in east Hampshire and Berkshire. Finally, there is a further literal on page 68: it should read No 7783 and not 7787.